George Henry Peters

Impressions of a Journey round the World

including India, Burmah and Japan

George Henry Peters

Impressions of a Journey round the World
including India, Burmah and Japan

ISBN/EAN: 9783744730587

Printed in Europe, USA, Canada, Australia, Japan

Cover: Foto ©Andreas Hilbeck / pixelio.de

More available books at **www.hansebooks.com**

IMPRESSIONS

OF A

JOURNEY ROUND THE WORLD

INCLUDING

INDIA, BURMAH AND JAPAN.

BY

GEORGE HENRY PETERS.

LONDON:
WATERLOW AND SONS LIMITED, PRINTERS, LONDON WALL
1897.

PREFACE.

I HAVE not a little hesitation in committing to print anything so modest as the enclosed rough notes of a voyage round the world, the more so because from its title the reader may not unreasonably suppose that he is about to peruse a record of stirring incidents and exciting adventures. For such incidents this book will, I am afraid, be scanned in vain.

Like many another voyager I found considerable pleasure during my travels in keeping a daily record of impressions of scenes visited. These records at first intended merely for my own after-perusal, I have, at the wish of many friends promised shall appear in somewhat more permanent form.

As will be seen from the opening remarks of my first chapter, it is a matter of considerable doubt in my own mind whether so uneventful a tour as this will prove of interest to the general reader; although perhaps to some, the description given of a few of the finest and most wonderful spots in the world may be welcome, if only as a pleasant stimulus to the recollection of impressions, formerly strong, but now becoming faint, of visits paid to many of the places described in the chapters of this book.

The diary form is observed almost throughout, for while I am well aware that it has many drawbacks when endeavouring to connect the events recorded with a running thread of interest, it lends itself, in my judgment, to a more accurate description both of the events taking place and also of the impressions received from the scenery and people visited.

The hesitation which I have felt in placing my "impressions of a journey round the world" in printed form is, perhaps, the best explanation I can give for the time which has elapsed since the date of my tour and the publication of this little volume.

GEO. HENRY PETERS.

LONDON, *December*, 1896.

CONTENTS.

PAGE

CHAPTER I. I

Departure from Southampton—In the Channel—"The Bay"—The Mediterranean — Genoa—Straits of Messina—Crete—Port Said—Suez Canal — Red Sea — Aden—Indian Ocean — Arrival at Ceylon.

CHAPTER II. 30

Landing in Colombo—Colombo "en fete"—The Tropical Vegetation, &c. — Description of Colombo — Mount Lavinia — Victoria Park, Colombo—To Kandy by Railway—Kandy—Peridenia Gardens—Tea Plantation—Buddha Tooth—Elephants—Newara Eliya—Return to Colombo—Departure for Bombay.

b

CHAPTER III. 60

Bombay Harbour—Bombay—The Towers of Silence—The Caves of Elephanta—Public Buildings—By Rail to Ahmedebad—Ahmedebad—Ajmere—Jeypore—Elephant Riding—Ambere—Delhi—Old Delhi—Agra—The Taj Mahal—Futtehpore Sikri—Secundara.

CHAPTER IV. 100

Indian Bird Life—Hindoo Marriage—Native Bazaar in Agra—Cawnpore—Sites of the Massacre—Memorial Well—Lucknow—The Residency—The Great Imambarah—Benares—The Monkey Temple — Cremation — Bathing in Ganges—Calcutta—River Hooghly.

CHAPTER V. 133

Burmah—Mandalay—The Mingoon Bell—River Irrawaddy — Pagan — Prome — Rangoon—The Golden Pagoda—S.S. Pentakota—Moulmein—Penang—Singapore.

CHAPTER VI. 160

China Sea — Hong Kong—Canton—Its Life—Macao—Fantan at Macao—Home of Luiz de Camoens — Return to Hong Kong — Pidgin English—Chinese Theatre—Poetry—Departure for Shanghai — Shanghai — China Town in Shanghai.

CHAPTER VII. 203

Arrival in Japan—Nagasaki—The Inland Sea—Kobe—Ozaka—Nara—Kegura Dance—Jinricksha to Kyoto—Kyoto—Yaamis' Hotel – Geisha Dance.

CHAPTER VIII. 233

Kyoto and its Temples—Cloisonné—Descent of the Rapids — Lake Biwa —Odzu—Nagoya—Fujiama — Yokohama —Miyanoshita—Tokio—Nikko and its wonderful Temples—Return to Yokohama—Dai Buku at Kamakura.

CHAPTER IX. 272

Japanese Literature—English as it is Japped—Optimistic and Pessimistic views of Japan—The Sandwich Islands—The Volcano Kilauea.

CHAPTER X. 294

Off to San Francisco—The Yosemite Valley—Salt Lake City—Chicago and the World's Fair—New York—Departure for England.

CONCLUSION 358

APPENDIX—(Buddha and Buddhism) . . . 361

# IMPRESSIONS

OF A

JOURNEY ROUND THE WORLD

(INCLUDING INDIA, BURMAH AND JAPAN).

CHAPTER I.

"Roll on, thou deep and dark blue Ocean—roll:
Ten thousand fleets sweep over thee in vain:
Man marks the earth with rain—his control
Stops with the shore; upon the watery plain
The wrecks are all thy deed, nor doth remain
A shadow of man's ravage; save his own,
When, for a moment, like a drop of rain
He sinks into the depth with bubbling groan,
Without a grave, unknelled, uncoffined, and unknown."—
LORD BYRON.

DEPARTURE FROM SOUTHAMPTON— IN THE CHANNEL— THE BAY — THE MEDITERRANEAN — GENOA — STRAITS OF MESSINA—CRETE—PORT SAID—SUEZ CANAL— RED SEA—ADEN—INDIAN OCEAN—ARRIVAL AT CEYLON.

IS it in these days an impossibility to write a simple record of travel that will amuse and interest the *blasé fin de siècle* reader? Is the public taste so vitiated and impregnated with Zolaism that nothing but excitability, realism and sensationalism will please? If so, this work had better be thrown aside, for the reader will find nothing suited to his palate.

It was on the morning of Sunday, December 11th, 1892, that I stepped on board His Imperial Majesty's Mail Steamer " Preussen," of 4,650 tons, owned by the North German Lloyd Company of Bremen, and bound with first, second, and even *two* third class passengers, for Genoa, Port Said, Aden, Colombo, Singapore, Hong Kong, and Shanghai.

The vessel was anchored for a few hours at the entrance to Southampton Water, and the passengers from England were conveyed to it from the Docks by a small steam tender. As my brother and I ran up the companion ladder the ship's band was already on deck, endeavouring by its inspiriting music to relieve the sadness of parting with those leaving for foreign lands from which they would never return, as well as with those embarking for health or pleasure. It was a cold, bright, winter's morning, but not too cold to prevent one being able to remain on deck and see the last of old England's chalky cliffs, which happened to be those of the Bill of Portland. We ran quickly through the narrow passage of the Needles, just giving a glance at the coloured sands of Alum Bay, and then heading straight for sea, were soon in the chops of the Channel. Over the next two days, or rather one night and one day, I will draw a veil, for were we not in the Bay of Biscay, experiencing one of its frequent gales and gaining a practical acquaintance with an "Atlantic roll"? The fish and the sad sea waves know more about our trouble than our gentle readers must. In fact, in Gilbertian phraseology, we "sought the seclusion that a cabin grants." The chief Lord of the Admiralty, impersonated by Mr. Grossmith in *H.M.S. "Pinafore,"* danced after singing the song of which the above is an extract, but we neither danced nor sang, but remained " uncomfortably down below." On Tuesday, the 13th, the wind had moderated and soon after passing Cape Finisterre, the sea had subsided sufficiently to allow us to take a little more interest in the world around us. In the evening the coast of Spain came into view, and the next morning we were basking in brilliant sunshine, the sea almost without a ripple, while shoals of porpoises were disporting themselves close by us. Our sea legs were now "on," and friendly intercourse with our fellow passengers commenced.

The Captain is one of the suave, polite German type, and is a great favourite. Under his especial protection is an attractive Fräulein, proceeding to Samoa to be married there; she is quite a heroine on board and has been nicknamed the "Princess of Samoa." It is a "far cry" there, and she will be two months *en route*. Thursday, the 15th inst., we passed close to the lighthouse on Cape St. Vincent, and keeping close to the Spanish coast all day, passed through the Straits of Gibraltar at night. Time now slipped away pleasantly on board; ship's billiards, quoits, cricket, music, with the occasional excitement of watching passing vessels at a distance and speculating as to their size, ownership and destination, being among the principal attractions of a sea voyage. On the morning of the 16th we came in sight of the Balearic Islands on our right. First came the smallest one, Iviza, then the large one of Majorca with its purple tinted mountains, and afterwards Minorca. For a few hours the whole range of the Sierra Nevadas, with the higher peaks covered with snow, was visible; and on Saturday morning, after running across the Gulf of Lyons through the night, the Riviera Coast off Toulon was sighted, with the Alpes Maritimes in the background. About midnight Genoa, the "City of Palaces," was reached. Although this Italian city had several times been previously visited by us, yet we did not fail to again see some of the principal sights; it is aptly called "Genoa the Superb," for its situation is unrivalled. It is built upon the sides of steep mountains descending to the Gulf of Genoa in the form of an amphitheatre, and viewed from the harbour at night, with its thousands of lights rising tier upon tier, it presented a beautiful scene. The most interesting street is the Via Nuovo, containing many marble palaces, the most noteworthy of which are the

Municipalio, in which Paganini's celebrated violin and the city's archives are preserved; and the Pallazzo Rosso, bequeathed to the city by the late Archduchess Galliera. This latter palace has a fine collection of oil paintings by celebrated masters. The interiors of the churches of St. Annunziata and St. Lorenzo are gorgeously decorated, and they possess fine marble and mural decorations. The white marble statue of Christopher Columbus standing in an open square near the railway station, and the gigantic cemetery, situated a few miles from the city, outside the walls, are worth visiting.

On Monday, the 19th, anchor was weighed, and we glided quietly out into the beautiful dark blue waters of the Mediterranean, heading for the far East. Late the same evening the lighthouse erected on the north-east coast of the Island of Corsica was plainly seen.

Four days were spent in splendid weather, with the exception of Thursday, 22nd, when we had a rolling sea for a few hours on passing the mouth of the Adriatic, and afterwards close to the Island of Candia, the ancient Crete. The narrow straits of Messina were passed on Wednesday morning at eight o'clock, but Etna was under cloud and we could only see the fair city of Messina. On the opposite side was the rugged mountainous coast of Calabria, with the pretty little town of Reggio nestling under the rocks. On the 24th, a high lighthouse was seen in the far distance right ahead of us, and in a few hours we were soon moored alongside the spacious quay and close to the offices of the different companies of ocean liners, the hotels and the shops, at Port Said.

As our vessel was obliged to wait for mails, (delayed by bad weather), it was decided that Christmas Eve should be spent in the usual German fashion, which is celebrated in the Fatherland with festivities of a very jovial character, and in a much more thorough manner than it is in England. Port Said would be the last place on earth that one would wish to spend Christmas in, but it was our fate to do so. The few ladies on board had organised a committee and had been very busy and mysterious all day, but we only fully understood after dinner what their arduous labours had been. A magnificently decorated Christmas tree, brilliantly illuminated, was unveiled in the dining saloon, and beside it sat the "Princess of Samoa," disguised as Santa Claus; who, rising at our entrance, welcomed us, with a recitation of quaint verses composed for the occasion, and immediately afterwards produced from a sack novel and unique presents for the passengers and officers of the ship. The second class passengers had been invited to be present, and we enjoyed some excellent music and choral singing. Later in the evening, to the surprise of the company, the saloon doors were thrown open and in marched a splendid representation of a camel, followed by the three wise men of the East, bearing cushions on which ornaments, etc., representing precious stones were placed. The procession passed slowly round the saloon three times and then departed. We discovered later that the camel was impersonated, much to their credit, by two of the stewards. The morning of Christmas Day was spent idling about the shops and stores of Port Said, providing ourselves with sundry necessaries in the way of cigarettes, and light pith hats for our journey through the Red Sea; also riding on donkeys, in Eastern style, to visit the native Arab village situated some distance from the modern town.

Port Said has an unenviable reputation, as it is essentially a town sprung into existence by the opening of the Suez Canal, and only a few years ago was non-existent. It consists principally of low-class cafés and gaming saloons, where an inferior kind of Monte Carlo "rouge et noir" is played. These cafés are frequented mostly by the sailors from the different ships anchoring in the harbour.

The magnificent work of the Suez Canal, connecting the Mediterranean with the Gulf of Suez and the Red Sea, has transformed the whole locality. It is a wonderful waterway and teems with interest different to that of any other canal, strait, or in fact any other similar piece of water in the world. As we enter the narrow channel one sees nothing but sand, and as far as the eye can reach stretches the pathless desert with occasional oases of rock and low hills. Close to us, in one of the sidings or stopping basins, is an Orient liner, bound for England from Australia; now we pass a hired transport outward bound to India and filled with British soldiers, who, give us a hearty British cheer as we come abreast of them. As we carry European mails to the East we are allowed to take precedence. At anchor at the canal entrance is a Messageries Maritimes liner bound for Jaffa and the Orient, and close to her a spruce English gun boat. Lazily, Egyptian fishing craft with quaintly shaped sails, and bright with the picturesque colouring of the costumes worn by the men, glide by; and slowly along the bank, following for a time our line of route, a long caravan of camels comes into view. Thus we are shown, at one time, through the medium of this artificial waterway, both Eastern life and Western civilisation.

At intervals neat signal stations are to be seen on the banks, with clean houses in the French style, and surrounded by little patches of garden, which break the monotony of the sandy desert land, and upon which foxes, wolves, and even lions, have been known to prowl. At each end of the canal, viz., at Port Said and at Suez, interesting charts can be seen in the offices of the Company, showing the exact position of each ship passing through the canal, the knowledge being conveyed from the station masters by telegraph. Large black balls or cones are also pulled up and down high signal posts to warn vessels of the approach of others in the contrary direction. The journey occupied eighteen hours, and the effect at night was weird in the extreme. A powerful electric search light was suspended from the head-mast, illumining the water and banks for a quarter of a mile, and about half a mile behind us the light of the troopship following us could be seen. A few years ago vessels were not allowed to proceed through the canal at night, but since the introduction and general use on board ship of the electric light, an enormous increase of business has resulted. The charge for the passage of a ship of this tonnage—4,650 tons—was something like £1,500, so it seems rather difficult to comprehend how this German Company can afford to pay such a tax unless they are handsomely subsidized by the paternal Government, which I believe is the case. About six o'clock in the evening we stopped for a very short time off Ismaila, the usual landing place *en route* for Cairo.

We had originally intended to break our journey here, but being so comfortable on board ship, and my brother having stayed at Cairo and seen the surroundings on a previous trip, when he visited Palestine, we determined to continue on board as far as Ceylon. Suez was passed at night, and early on the morning of December 27th, we found ourselves in the Gulf of Suez, and surrounded by arid, rocky mountains of a light brown colour. Presently on our left the Sinaitic range came into view. Mount Sinai itself is, I think, not to be seen, although the highest peak of the range visible from the sea is pointed out as the Holy Mountain. The Gulf of Suez forms part of, and is, in fact, an integral portion of, the Red Sea, the waters of which are of an ultramarine tint, and rival the blue of the Mediterranean. Land is only observable at intervals, so the passage of the Israelites out of Egypt must have taken place more in the neighbourhood of the Bitter Lakes, before the deepened channel was made to allow vessels to cross them, and where at certain periods the wind has been known to blow the water out into the Gulf of Suez, thus leaving the bottoms of the lakes dry.

On the afternoon of December 28th, the Tropic of Cancer was passed, which Captain Högemann endeavoured to point out, by cunningly placing a hair across the glass of the ship's telescope, to some of the lady passengers, one of whom declared that she saw "it" distinctly! In the evening we experienced our first tropical sunset. To the Westward extended a long line of mountains with serrated peaks, and behind them the golden orb slowly sank, bringing out into strong relief against the sky line the fantastic curves of the range and their beautiful jagged peaks; slowly over the waters a purple hue spread itself, and as the sun disappeared, with the heavens all glowing, the colour of the water deepened, and we saw the Red Sea before us in reality.

The weather through the Red Sea was changeable. On the first two days we had glorious weather, with our first experience of a tropical sun, and a calm sea. It was so intensely hot that we remained under the awnings on deck until two o'clock in the morning, to make our nights down below pass more quickly; but on the third day the wind became southerly and there was a great deal of motion.

On the 30th we passed twelve rocky islets, called "The Apostles," and during the night ran through the Straits of Babelmandeb. In the afternoon of the following day we anchored off our British possession of Aden for a few hours to take in water preparatory to continuing the voyage across the Arabian Sea and Indian Ocean to Ceylon.

Aden is very interesting to the European, and one is amused, immediately after anchoring, by watching Arab boys surrounding the vessel, paddling in small canoes hollowed out of the trunks of trees. They commence by shouting " Have a dive, have a dive! oio, oie, oie, oio! *à la mer, à la mer*! good boy, good boy!" which is followed, upon a small coin being thrown into the water, by the speedy abandonment of paddle and canoe, on the part of the boy. He has dived out of sight, but reappears in a second or two with the coin between his teeth, and immediately swims after his abandoned canoe and paddle. These lads are very dexterous divers, and the cadence of their voices is rather pleasing to the ear. Sharks are very numerous at

Aden, and it is astonishing that no accidents happen, but even *sharks* do not appear to have a particular relish for young Arabs, and are more alive to the delicate eating of white men's flesh, for which they are generally on the *qui vive*. We spent two hours on shore, visiting the huge tanks, of which there are 50 in Aden, and which, if cleared out, would have an average capacity of 30,000,000 gallons. A Mr. Salt, who saw them in 1809, writes: " The most remarkable of these reservoirs consists of a line of cisterns situated on the north side of the town, three of which are fully 80 feet wide, and proportionately deep, all executed out of the solid rock, and lined with a thick coat of fine stucco." In 1856, the restoration of these magnificent tanks was undertaken by Capt. F. M. Hunter. To reach these cisterns we hired light carriages at the landing place, and after passing a crescent of shops, we drove across a sandy plain, then ascended a steep hill in zigzags, and passed through a fortified cutting at the top, which divides the fortress of Aden from the town itself. On the sea shore, several Mahommedans turned towards Mecca, were devoutly praying, with their foreheads bowed; and we constantly met numbers of camels carrying heavy loads of wood and sacks filled with rice. The old Arab town was then reached, in which, the people, goats, camels, fowls, etc., were seen all living comfortably together. On reaching the tanks, we found to our surprise, that they were beautifully clean, and had not contained any water for seven years; indeed, I was told it has not rained at Aden for that period. A few trees and shrubs had been planted by the English, and the whole place was in the charge of three native soldiers. With the exception of the green leaves of the shrubs above mentioned, not a blade of grass of any kind was observable. Aden is situated on a promontory of high hills, covered with brown rocks and sands, while the modern town nestles round a bay on the eastern side. Apart from its Asiatic character, which pleased us, the whole place is hot, arid and uninviting.

As we steamed away, the North German Lloyd Steamer, "Darmstadt" arrived from Shanghai, and saluted her sister ship, as we passed almost abreast. The bands of both ships played, and enthusiastic cheering and waving of handkerchiefs took place.

December 31*st*. This is the last night of the old year, and by a cordial invitation from the second class passengers, we are asked to spend it with them, in return for the entertainment given by the first class cabin on Christmas Eve. New Year's Eve will be thus spent at sea, in the Gulf of Aden, out of sight of land, which we shall not see again for seven days, unless we happen to sight the island of Socotra, about 150 miles East of Cape Guardafui (which is the Eastern point of the African continent), or any of the respective groups of the Laccadive or Maldive Islands off the West coast of the Southern portion of our Indian Empire. The thoughts of officers, passengers and crew will naturally be with the dear ones at home, who will themselves be thinking of the absent ones; and from our hearts, we send them this message from the sea,—" Good health, Happiness and a Bright New Year!"

Sunday morning, January 1st, 1893. Last night's entertainment was a great success, and everybody enjoyed the "Sylvester Abend." A procession was formed, headed by the band, and we proceeded through the length and breadth of the ship, along the principal gangways and decks to a temporary ball room arranged on the port side of the hurricane deck. This was made gay with lanterns and bunting, and also by the electric light, which is used in every part of the ship. Here we danced the sprightly polka, the giddy valse and the ceremonious lancers, and when tired with terpsichorean charms, champagne bowl refreshed the inner man and was also sipped by gentler lips. Then at the witching hour of midnight, silence stole over us while once more an old year passed away and a new one began, to the solemn tolling of the ship's bell and the firing of guns. The band then played a suitable choralé, and after mutual congratulations our pleasant evening ended.

Sunday evening at sea. The vault of the sky is of a grey colour, just flecked to the eastward with a few fleecy clouds, and the ocean slumbering and looking like a painted sheet of dark blue canvas; there is no noise but the occasional splash of the water receding after contact with the vessel's prow, and turning over into gentle waves of white foam, and yet we are sailing in the teeth of a north-east monsoon. This may sound terrible to a land lubber, but the result is in reality very pleasant. A westerly or south-westerly monsoon would mean a high sea sweeping over decks, scorching heat, and an unpleasant rolling of the ship; but the accompaniments of a north-easter are a cool, pleasant breeze, a placid sea with the gentle waves just curling here and there into white foam, over which one sees occasional flights of flying fish, looking like small aquatic birds skimming over the waters. This fish is about the size of a mackerel, with two small wings fixed near the head; it has a black back and looks much more like a bird until you see it disappearing with a little splash into the waves.

January 2nd.—For two hours this morning we have been passing the mountainous Island of Socotra, about four miles to the westward; in fact at one time it seemed we were not more than a mile away. This is a British possession subordinate to Aden, but administered in its internal affairs by its own chiefs. What appeared at first to be a large glacier descending between two mountains into the sea, proves on closer inspection to be a bed of pure white sand stretching towards the sea in the form of a fan. At Aden we took on board a party of Malays from Singapore, who were returning from a pilgrimage to the shrine of Mahomet at Mecca. There are twenty-three in all, men and boys, and they are not berthed but are simply lying on their red and blue flannel shawls on the foredeck in close proximity to the live stock, consisting of oxen, sheep, pigs, calves, turkeys, geese, fowls, ducks, etc. They live upon curried rice and dates mostly, and between meals are always smoking the chibouque. Their manner of eating is very noticeable. After seating themselves in a circle with their legs crossed under them, a wooden bowl of the boiled rice is placed in the centre; the elder then first puts his hand into the dish and takes out a handful, which is formed into a compact mass by pressing it with his palms and fingers. This delicacy he then inserts into his mouth, throwing back the remaining crumbs into the bowl. All the other members then go through the same form until the bowl is empty. They are very devout, and at sunset, with their faces turned towards Mecca, alternately standing with folded hands, and kneeling with the forehead touching the deck in lieu of mother earth, they muttered their prayers.

Friday, January 5th.—This is the sixth day at sea since our departure from Aden, and up to the present we have seen no natural green of any kind. We are now, however, nearing the Island of Minacoy, one of the Laccadive group, the Chief of which goes yearly to Ceylon to pay reverence to Her Majesty's representative, and also to receive for this act of obeisance the sum of 5,000 rupees. Across the horizon to the leeward we soon perceive a few palm trees, and in half-an-hour we are sailing by the beautiful island. Before us we have a real tropical coral island, surrounded by reefs over which a long line of surf is breaking, while behind it rise forests of palm trees. At the nearest point to us is a high lighthouse, and one of the duties of the native chief is to see that the revolving light in it is kept burning. The coral reef is within half-a-mile of us, so we have a glorious view of this gem set in the deep blue of the Indian Ocean.

To-day an international cricket match has taken place on our ship — "Germany *versus* England." Twelve stalwart Germans and two ladies against four English, and the result ended in the ignominious defeat of the Teuton on his own deck. In justice to our opponents I must admit that they had never played before, and that we were the challengers. The Germans were practising at six o'clock in the morning. The score was as follows:—

GERMANY.	Runs.	ENGLAND.	Runs.
First Innings	... 7	First Innings (retired)	... 29
Second Innings	... 12	Second Innings	... —
Total	... 19	Total	... 29

England retired with her laurels, winning by

an innings and ten runs. Capt. Högemann was bowled out first ball, the first lieutenant scored four, while the "Princess of Samoa" gained great applause by obtaining four also. At the conclusion of the match international courtesies were indulged in, the Germans proceeding to the smoking-room to recoup exhausted nature by the imbibition of sundry cocktails, and the English refreshing themselves with draughts of Lager Beer.

Last day at sea.—We were awakened at two o'clock in the morning by a grating noise of the ship's screw, and discovered on rising later that one of the plates had broken; but we proceeded on our voyage quite safely, though the vessel was rolling throughout the day. About three o'clock the mountains of Ceylon were sighted, and in a glorious sunset we entered and dropped anchor in the Harbour of Colombo.

CHAPTER II.

Landing in Colombo—Colombo "en fête"—The Tropical Vegetation, &c.—Description of Colombo — Mount Lavinia — Victoria Park, Colombo — To Kandy by Railway — Kandy — Peridenia Gardens — Tea Plantation — Buddha Tooth — Elephants—Newara Eliya—Return to Colombo—Departure for Bombay.

COLOMBO possesses a fine artificial harbour and breakwater, the first stone of which was laid by H.R.H. the Prince of Wales in 1874. At the extreme end of the breakwater stands a lighthouse, visible 18 miles away at sea. We were anchored next to an Austrian man-of-war, engaged at present in the pleasant occupation of taking the Austrian Crown

Prince on a tour round the world. On landing, we found the town *en fête* and decorated in honour of the Crown Prince's visit, with triumphal arches made of bamboo canes thatched with palm leaves, from which the fruits of the jak tree, bread fruit and cocoanut trees were hanging. The Island of Ceylon has been variously styled the Garden of Eden, Paradise, and the Spicy Isle; the latter term because of the powerful scent of the clove and cinnamon trees, wafted out to sea when the wind is blowing from the land. The brilliant colouring of the luxuriant vegetation and the red soil, the forests of palms and glorious fruits and flowers, all tend to charm the traveller and to entrance his imagination. After we had landed we were at once taken in waggonettes, called "gharries," and drawn by small horses to the Galle Face hotel, facing the sea and about a mile and a half outside the town. Our luggage followed in a cart with a covering of dried palm leaves, and drawn by a pair of native "Zebu," or bulls. This animal resembles our own bullock, but with the addition of a large hump on the back, just behind the horns, and is used by the natives all over the island. The hotel is more of the bungalow type, quiet and comfortable, with a lovely view of the sea. This place, in a few years, bids fairly to become the ocean's "Clapham Junction," situated as it is, midway between the East and West. Day by day steamers pass, going to or returning from China or Australia, and if a dockyard were built, Colombo would quickly become the most important Naval Station in the Orient. Close to the hotel is a breezy expanse of common, while in the gardens large cocoa nut trees are growing, and under their fronds large clusters of green fruit are hanging. In a few minutes we can be conveyed in a "jinricksha" into the heart of the town. The "jinricksha" is a two-wheeled carriage, somewhat resembling a bath chair, but higher, and with a hood to protect the occupier from the sun. It is drawn by native coolies, who run, perspiring at every pore, between small shafts. Ceylon is famous for its crows, called "Nature's scavengers." They are cheeky fellows, and this morning at six o'clock, two of them appeared at my open window, and hopped in on to the chota hazri, or early breakfast table, and made off with the toast. Their plumage is quite black, but they have glossy purple wings. Soon after breakfast, following the morning of our arrival, we were off across the common to pay our first visit to the city. On rising ground we noticed the club house, a handsome two storied building, built of course in bungalow style, and close to it was the pretty English church, fitted with punkahs, which are pulled by boys standing in the porchways. There is a great misnomer in calling one's servant a boy, as he need not be young. A patriarchal looking man asked us in the hotel this morning, if we required a boy during our stay in Ceylon, and when we asked him to produce him, he said that *he* was the boy! We proceeded past a splendid lake, winding through the centre of Colombo, the banks of which were fringed with palms, while the beautiful hibiscus with its gorgeous crimson blossoms as large as camellias, were seen growing in abundance. To the left of the lake are the English barracks, built with open archwork of solid stone, and near them the residence of the Governor. The European quarter which is near the sea-shore, has fine broad streets, with avenues of trees, while the native quarter is almost hidden by the forests of palm trees. The Pettah quarter is the most interesting, and here the natives were to be seen sitting in the doorways of their thatched huts, while the roads swarmed with the people in all varieties of coloured costumes. Our first drive was to Mount Lavinia, about seven miles distant, situated on a small bay. Long streets of native huts and shops, in which all kinds of dried fish, bananas, cocoa-nuts, mangoes and rice were exposed for sale, were passed. The Singhalese are very cleanly in their habits, and we noticed mothers washing their healthy, plump babies with soap and water. The men are very proud of their black hair, which is not cut, but combed back carefully from the forehead and tied in a small knot or chignon at the back of the head, while on the top a tortoise shell comb shaped to the head is worn. The food of the people consists of fish in large quantities, rice, curry, cocoanut, the fruit of the bread fruit, etc., and they looked strong and healthy on this diet. As we drove along we passed through groves of cocoa-nut palm trees with huge clusters of the fruit hanging far out of our reach. This latter tree is certainly one of the most useful in the world. The natives build their houses and make carts and furniture with its wood; its fronds when dry are used for thatching their roofs and making coverings for their bullock carts; its fruits they subsist on and the husks are used for making coir ropes and matting as well as fuel. As we drove on we noticed banana plantations and the jak fruit tree with its curious fruit growing on the trunks of the trees. This fruit is so heavy, weighing sometimes 20 lbs., that it could not possibly grow on the branches. Breadfruit trees crowded with the unripe and green fruit, and remarkable for the size of their leaves, measuring from $1\frac{1}{2}$ to 2 feet in length; giant bamboo trees, (*Dendrocalamus giganteus*), the canes of which attain to such a size that they are used as masts for fishing luggers; the banyan tree with the branches growing downwards and into the earth again, the talipot palm, the catalpa, the mango with its delicious yellow fruit; magnificent variegated crotons, six to eight feet in height; giant poinsettias with their scarlet foliage were all passed in bewildering succession, until we arrived at our destination. Here we found a modern hotel situated on a small hill, with a terrace commanding a fine sea view, where we partook of our first "tiffin." The menu was so elaborate, and so good, that I am tempted to give it "*in toto.*"

MOUNT LAVINIA HOTEL,

Sunday, January 8th, 1893.

TIFFIN :—

Native Oysters.

Turtle Soup.

Filets of Sole á la Maitre d'Hotel.

Devilled Whitebait.

Scalloped Oysters.

French Salad.

Mutton Cutlets á la Jardiniére.

Game Pie.

Marrow Patties.

Ice Pudding.

Bananas, Pine Apples.

Ginger.

Coffee.

I am sure this déjeuner would have pleased the most fastidious Parisian gourmet. After this repast we strolled out into the gardens, which sloped to the sea shore and where native boys were fishing. Fish of all kinds abound in these waters and men are constantly to be seen, standing on the golden sands, fishing with a rod in the surf and catching plenty of fish. Roughly hewn canoes with long outriggers are used, called catamarans, which ride easily over the surf into the calm deep water beyond. Strolling round the gardens we notice a stately silver crane with spotted breast, standing so quietly that we imagined it to be of porcelain. Amongst the flowers were the four o'clock flower, blooming only at four o'clock, the *bougainvillea spectabilis*, with its gorgeous sprays of purple blossom, and the waxen fragrant *frangipanni*, or temple flower, about the size of a chestnut growing in clusters on trees. This flower is of delicate wax, with a tinge of yellow, and is offered in the Buddhist temples by the natives; hence its name. It is similar to the tube-rose but more beautiful.

On the return journey we visited a small Buddhist temple, with one recumbent figure of Gautama, 25 feet long, in a glass case. Buddhists are not like the Mahommedan and Hindoo, who refuse Christians to enter into their inner sanctuaries, and one is allowed to visit all parts of Buddhist temples. Close to the temple were several priests, sitting in their huts. They are celibate, but believe for their act of renunciation on earth, to enjoy the blessings of perfect connubial bliss in the hereafter, and as a solace to their feelings a rude representation of a charming lady, showing a healthy babe to its father, was hanging from the ceiling of the temple above the heads of the priests. These priests, like most of the Singhalese, have an objectionable habit of chewing a mixture of betel nut, areca palm and tobacco leaf, which turns their teeth to a hideous red colour giving the appearance of bleeding when their mouths are opened, and spoiling the otherwise pearly whiteness of their teeth. Leaving the temple we drove on to the beautiful park called "Victoria," after our Queen. There were golfing grounds, tennis court enclosures, a riding ground and beautiful gardens, with variegated crotons, dracænas, acacias and other flowering trees. The allamanda, so admired in English hot-houses, was growing here as a parasite on other trees, with hundreds of yellow blossoms. Then through the Cinnamon Gardens back to our hotel.

This morning, January 8th, we saw an exhibition of snake charming with two cobra capellas. The instrument used by the charmer is called a Mughidi, a Tamil word, signifying a decoy or charm. The mughidi had certainly a great effect upon the reptiles, for when first brought out of their baskets they were easily excited, but eventually coiled themselves round the neck of the man, exhibiting their fangs but without attempting to bite. Then we made a round of the Bazaars. The principal objects of interest are, ebony wood carving, cheap white and blue sapphires, boxes made of sandal wood and boxes with the sides and lids made from the quills of the porcupine. The natives have a superstition that the fates will be propitious to them during the day if they sell cheaply in the morning; it is always as well then to buy something from them at " Morning time, for Luck."

In the "Innocents Abroad," Mark Twain describes very graphically the monstrosities of poor misshapen human beings to be seen in Constantinople; and coming nearer home, Mr. Barnum exhibited a few hideous specimens at Olympia, but all these must pale before the wretched creature we have seen to-day. It bore the nearest resemblance to the monkey tribe possible. The man had an intelligent and expressive face with piercing black eyes, but his body was covered with thick black hair and he possessed a pair of long narrow hands, perfectly formed, but his arms were barely three inches long, and he was thereby prevented from touching his face with the former. It was a horrible sight, not easily forgotten.

This morning we ascended an artificially raised hill in the centre of the city, from the summit of which a superb view was to be obtained. To our surprise, with the exception of a few spires, Colombo was not to be seen, and yet we had only just quitted a city containing 130,000 inhabitants. All we really could see was a gigantic forest of palms under which the storied bungalows of the Europeans, the huts and shops of the natives were hidden, thus affording them a wonderful protection during the hot season from the scorching rays of the sun.

Starting at 1.55 from the principal railway station of the Ceylon Railway Company we were soon speeding, in a comfortable open saloon car, into the interior of the island. Close to Mahara station is the quarry from which the stone was brought for the formation of the huge breakwater at Colombo, and in close proximity to Henaratgoda are the Government Tropical Gardens containing many varieties of the caoutchouc or rubber giving trees, Trinidad cacao, Liberian coffee, and Gutta-percha trees from the Malay Peninsula. At this station, which was brilliant with crotons, we were offered by the aborigines, royal cocoanuts, bananas, pineapples, eggs, etc. After leaving the station the track slowly commenced to ascend, and a second engine was coupled on behind to push us up to the top of the pass, 1698 feet above sea level. Beautifully wooded knolls soon gave place to higher hills and mountains, while the vegetation increased in luxuriance.

After running along the sides of some precipitous mountains, affording magnificent views of the valley far beneath us, and noticing the increasing delicious coolness of the air, we reached the watershed. Here a column was erected to the memory of Capt. Dawson, the engineer of the first road. Just above the Station (Kadugannawa) is the Hill of Balungaola or the Watcher's Rock (2,543 feet). The companion engine was here uncoupled, and we commenced the descent, with a mountain torrent falling over rocks and stones accompanying us alongside; while above, the beautifully covered hills and peaks reminded one of a bit of Scotch or Swiss scenery; and we soon arrived at Kandy, the capital of the former kingdom of Kandy. Here also triumphal arches had been erected in honour of the Austrian Crown Prince who had gone on an elephant shooting expedition about five days distance. It was just dusk when we arrived, and thousands of fire-flies were flitting about in the air like small silver stars, while the chirping of grasshoppers was heard everywhere. Kandy contains a mixed population of 22,000, Singhalese, Tamils and Hindoos, and is situated 1,680 feet above the mean sea level in a narrow valley completely hemmed in by wooded hills and mountains, and it is the centre of the planting interest. The Queen's hotel, a large two-storied building, situated close to a large winding lake and by the side of an open green, upon which a local volunteer band was playing, received us.

January 12*th.*—This afternoon we spent in visiting a model tea plantation and factory, situated at Peridenia, about four miles distant. The tea plant is carefully pressed down to a uniform height of from two to three feet from the ground and has the appearance of a small bay tree, while its leaves are about the size of bay leaves. After plucking the fresh green leaves, "withering" is the first operation, and this takes place in large open airy rooms, where the leaves are spread out on layers of matting made from jute; when reduced to a silken texture and while still in a damp state, they are crushed in large rollers; drying then follows, by their being laid in large tin trays, which are placed in an ingenious machine, into which hot air is forced. Then the sifting and packing is accomplished, and the chests are ready for exportation. The smell of the factory reminded one of the strongest tea imaginable during the process of brewing. Near to this factory are the beautiful Botanical Gardens of Peridenia. Immediately upon entering, was to be seen a plantation of magnificent tropical palms, including specimens of the fan-shaped travellers' palm (*Ravenala Madagascariensis*), which if cut in a portion of the stalk, produces sufficient water for the thirsty traveller; the *Oscosperma fasciculata*, the oil palm of Ceylon; the *Lewistonia altissima*, the *Oreodoxia regia*, or cabbage palm; and the *talipot*, which blooms only once in a hundred years and then dies. Some of these palms were 90 feet high. Colossal banyan trees and fine specimens of the India-rubber tree (*Ficus elastica*) we then passed. The deadly Upas tree from Java, the allspice, giant bamboos with canes measuring 30 inches in diameter and 100 feet high, Java almonds, the clove and the nutmeg, both from 50 to 60 feet high; the cotton tree, covered with its red flowers, like those of the azalea, many sorts of the mango, and an avenue of 80 or 90 cabbage palms, 70 and 80 feet high, were all shown, Ceylon is more noted for its flowering creepers and trees, than for plants. The lantana shrub, the pale blue plumbago, the bragmansia or the trumpet flower, the poinsettia, the oleander, huge violet and white convolvuli, and the passiflora, grow in the jungle and by the wayside in a wild state. The two most interesting flowering trees are the *Amherstia Nobilis*, as large as a chestnut and bearing a lovely drooping red waxen orchid-like flower, and the *Napoleonis Imperialis*, with a small yellow flower, exactly the shape of the Imperial Napoleonic crown Every visitor to Ceylon should visit these gardens, which are arranged like a private park.

At 6.30 this evening we heard the weird

and unearthly beating of the tom-tom, from the Great Buddhist Temple, known as the Daladá Máligáwa or Temple of the Tooth, in which the sacred tooth of Buddha and other relics are preserved,—calling the faithful to prayers. The temple or pagoda is situated at the extreme end of the green It originally formed part of the ancient palace of the kings of Kandy, and is surrounded by a moat. After passing through one or two doorways, decorated with rude frescoes describing human sins on earth and the respective punishments awarded for each kind of crime, we entered the minor courtyards in the centre of which stood the temple adorner, with small tawdry flags and hanging oil-lamps. The door of the shrine was of brass repoussé work and was flanked by a pair of handsome elephants' tusks. Entering, we passed many dirty Buddhist beggars holding lighted pieces of candle, then ascended a steep wooden staircase on the right and into the sanctuary itself. Behind a strongly barred iron casement stood the solid golden bell-shaped shrine highly ornamented with precious stones and gems. There are six of these shrines placed one above each other, and under the smallest of them the tooth is preserved. It is about four inches long and is very seldom exhibited. In front of the case was an antique silver table, before which two toothless hideous priests stood, holding out a large silver salver for offerings; and, although according to the tenets of their religion they are not allowed to solicit alms, yet they had the effrontery to do so before the most holy of their relics. On the table, blossoms of the temple flower, with its incense-like scent, and of the tithonia, a common yellow flower, not unlike our single sunflowers, were strewn. The ceiling was covered with Indian silk, while over the shrine a silvered crown of lotus flowers was hanging.

January 14*th.*—This afternoon we started off to see the elephants in their native haunts. To do this, had long been a cherished wish of our hearts, so after driving for several miles, two Singhalese coolies were discovered, who, at our driver's request, disappeared into the jungle to drive the beasts in our direction. We then drove on until we arrived at some huts, near which a portion of the jungle had been cleared. Here then, at last was the spot where the elephants would surprise us with their trumpeting, and dash through the under-growth. As the cleared space seemed sufficiently guarded by palisading, we waited patiently the arrival of the beasts. In the meatime we strolled about and noticed pine apples, the areca nut, palm, bananas and other plants. Still the elephants did not appear and no sound of any kind reached us that any chance of their coming was near, when turning round, we discovered a solitary specimen who seemed perfectly subdued and tame, walking towards us down the lane from the direction whence we had come. It was a fine beast and his keeper kindly put him through the usual Zoological Garden kind of entertainment. Unfortunately we had brought no buns with us, but we gave the keeper one of the depreciated rupees. Only one other specimen did we see on our return, and this one was bathing himself about half a mile away in a river and looked sufficiently picturesque, but, alas, for our cherished illusions, he too, was a show, and placed there for us. It is of no use, we can get up no adventures. No leopards have sprung upon us in the jungle, and no deadly cobra capella or venomous tic polonga have buried their poisonous fangs in any tender part of our anatomy. But writing seriously; in the wilder parts of the island, the elephant, the cheetah or Ceylon leopard, the bear, the elk, monkey, wild cat, &c., as well as cobra capellas, and the tic polonga, whose bite is most deadly, are to be found. The shooting of the elephant is now forbidden, but a special drive was arranged for the Crown Prince, who succeeded (so say the papers) in bringing down two.

A beautiful drive near Kandy is called " Lady Horton's Drive." One ascends a wooded hill, through palm groves, in zigzags, until a plateau is reached from which an extensive view of the central mountains of Ceylon is obtained. Far below stretched the valley of Dumbala, through which the longest river in the island flowed, looking like a silver ribbon thrown on the green landscape. Huge and gorgeously coloured butterflies flitted about us like small birds, some of them measuring six to eight inches from wing to wing.

Newara Eliya, pronounced Newerelia, is a hill station in Ceylon, situated at an elevation of 6,200 feet above sea-level, and lies in an extensive undulating plateau, in the centre of which is a beautiful lake; while tennis courts, golf links, &c., surround the grounds of the Grand hotel. Here rhododendrons and mimosa flourish. This upland valley is reached by rail from Kandy to Nanuoya station (5,291 feet), passing along the sides of precipitous mountains and ravines, while the valleys below present a scene of tea cultivation, rivalling those of the vineyards in Germany and France. About ten years ago a fungus pest attacked the coffee plant, and the planters with praiseworthy perseverance and indomitable energy proceeded to cultivate the tea plant, and in this short time have succeeded in their enterprise.

The stumps of the deceased coffee trees can still be seen in the tea plantations. Huge flowering aloes grow by the sides of the railway, and are useful in protecting the plantations from predatory cattle. After arriving at Nanuoya station, waggonettes convey passengers on to Newara Eliya through a romantic pass, covered with jungle, in which splendid specimens of the woolly tree fern *(Alsophila crinita)* are growing, the foliage at the time of our visit wearing lovely autumnal tints. The whole of the valley reminds one of an upland English or Scotch scene, as we are thousands of feet above the land of the palm and banana. The bracing climate makes this one of the most frequented hill stations for Anglo-Indians in the tropics. At one part of the journey the sea, at a distance of 60 miles, as the crow flies, could be seen. Adam's peak, one of the most frequently ascended mountains in Ceylon, we observed on the right. The mountain is supposed to have an impress of Buddha's foot at its summit, and is ascended at certain periods by devout pilgrims. The highest mountain in Ceylon is named Pidurutalaga (Pedro), 8,295 feet, and is covered with trees and jungle to the summit. At Hakgalla, near Newara Eliya, are some botanical gardens, 6,000 feet above sea level. Here English flowers were growing in the open, as well as maiden hair ferns, and splendid tree ferns by hundreds, the most interesting of which, was the New Zealand silver tree fern, while cacti, prickly pears, and the camphor tree, were also pointed out to us.

January 16*th.*—We returned to Colombo to-day, being nine hours *en route*. On the journey we passed through plantations of cacao, with the large chocolate coloured pods, and of cinchona from which quinine is produced.

January 19*th.*—We are leaving Colombo this afternoon in the Peninsular and Oriental Company's mail steamer, "Malwa," bound for Bombay, 887 miles distant. The ship has been delayed in loading her cargo of tea in consequence of a severe tropical rainstorm, accompanied with lightning and thunder which broke over us last night, but all day long the chests were being lowered into the hold. The harbour is full of life and commotion, as there are several mail steamers in port. Quaintly shaped junks are sailing about, while catamaran canoes are conveying passengers to and fro. On the decks half a dozen Mahommedans are tempting the passengers with all kinds of Ceylonese stones, the best of which is the dark blue sapphire; rubies, white sapphires, catseyes, moonstones, opals and pearls are offered, and all are found on this island. This gives some form of credence to the idea that it was the island mentioned in the "Arabian Nights," as visited by Sindbad the Sailor. However, the signal is given to start, the natives dart down the companion, and weighing anchor we glide out into the Indian Ocean, which is without a ripple. For some time we watch the fair shore of the Spicy Isle, with its belted girdle of golden sands, and the picturesque background of the forest of palm trees until the view fades into the distance.

CHAPTER III.

Bombay Harbour—Bombay—The Towers of Silence—
The Caves of Elephanta—Public Buildings—By
Rail to Ahmedabad — Ahmedebad — Ajmère—
Jeypore—Elephant Riding—Ambère—Delhi—Old
Delhi—Agra—The Taj Mahal—Futtehpore Sikri—
Secundara.

AFTER three days' pleasant sail with continual glimpses of the Malabar Coast of our Indian Empire, about six miles off, we steamed into Bombay harbour, on Sunday afternoon, the 22nd of January. The city is built on one of a group of islands, separated from each other by very narrow channels.

Bombay island is 11½ miles long, and its area is about 22 square miles. The population is something like 804,500, and consists of Europeans, Hindoos of different castes, Mahommedans, Parsees, Tamils and others. On approaching Bombay, to the right were to be seen red tinted hills rising from 1,000 to 2,000 feet from the sea. The highest point of Bombay island itself, is only 180 feet high, and is called Malabar hill. This hill is covered with charming bungalows and gardens. The harbour was at the time of our arrival crowded with vessels of all types, English men of war, merchant ships, Indian dhows and fishing boats. Immediately after anchoring, we noticed several boats approaching the ship's side, full of gorgeously attired Hindoos, carrying garlands and wreaths of flowers, and soon discovered that they were a committee of reception of the Thakore of Gonda, who had been a fellow passenger on board from Colombo, and was returning to India from a voyage round the world. The reception was novel. The members of the deputation advanced and in saluting His Highness, threw the wreaths and garlands round his neck, while silver rupees were strewn at his feet. We hardly thought the latter necessary, as the Thakore is reputed to be worth twelve lakhs of rupees. He is an intellectual man, and was educated at Edinburgh University.

We landed shortly after at the Apollo Bunder pier, close to which are the grounds of the Yacht Club, where the band plays before dinner, the Club being one of the rendezvous of Bombay society.

January 23*rd*. After breakfast we had our first walk. The groupings of handsome buildings, the large open squares and public gardens, boulevards planted with fine trees, tend to make modern Bombay the finest city in the East. In the native or "Bhendi" quarter, the streets are mostly narrow but very clean and bright and they teem with Oriental life. The quaint bullock carts loaded with cotton, and the crowds of people, coming and going, some in gay dresses and handsome turbans and some in next to nothing at all, remind one of the constant changes of the kaleidoscope. Arabs, Parsees, Persians, Afghans, Malays, Chinese, Jews, Fakirs, Mahommedans, are all to be seen. The Crawford market was founded by Mr. Arthur Crawford, C.S., and consists of a large central hall, in which is a drinking fountain given by Sir Cowasje Zchanger Readymoney, surmounted by a tower rising 128 feet high. To the right is a wing filled with beautiful fruits, viz.: golden or red bananas, or plantains as they are known in the East, oranges, melons, Bombay mangoes, pomegranates, tomatoes, all arranged most temptingly. Outside the wing is the fruit mart and auction mart, and the bird section. Parrots, paroquets, canaries, etc., were the principal varieties; as many as fifty birds being in one cage together. On the left is another wing 350 feet long by 100, for vegetables and spices, and surrounding these halls are fine gardens in which the meat and fish pavilions are built. The whole market is a model of cleanliness and cost over 1,000,000 rupees. We next visited the cotton market. Cotton spinning has developed very considerably during the last few years in Bombay and there are now 59,000 hands employed in the mills and 7,000,000 cwt. of cotton is exported annually. After tiffin we drove along the Mayo road, the right side of which, is an Appian way of magnificent edifices, including the Presidential Secretariat, the University, library and clock tower, the University hall, the Courts of Justice, the Post Office and the Telegraph Office, all standing in private grounds; while on the left, is the beautiful Back bay, with the Malabar hill in the distance, to which we were bound. On the summit of the hill stands the celebrated tower of Silence. These towers are used as burial places by the Parsees, who are Zoroastrians, and as they reverence the sun, fire, earth, and water, they have devised the means of disposing of their dead by placing the corpses in one of these huge towers, which are cylindrical in shape and white washed. The largest cost £30,000, is 276 feet round and is open to the sky. Inside, the plan of the building resembles somewhat an amphitheatre, with compartments for the male, female and children's bodies, all radiating from the centre. The bodies are placed in these grooves quite naked, and in half-an-hour the flesh is completely devoured by the ravenous vultures, flying about and resting in the neighbouring trees. The bones are left to bleach in the sun, and when dry, the carriers of the dead remove them and cast them into the centre well. The Parsees reverence the dead, but consider corpses unclean, and therefore the carriers are not allowed to associate with other Parsees. We saw large numbers of the voracious birds perched on the walls of one of the towers and waiting for the next arrival. It was a revolting sight to notice the birds returning gorged from the human feast with their beaks and breasts presenting a greasy appearance. While we were there, a funeral was taking place and the mourners were praying in an adjacent house of prayer. Around is a beautiful garden full of flowers, where relatives can sit and meditate, and are, or are not, disturbed in their meditations, according to their temperaments, by the flights of vultures, crows, etc., from one tower to another. Great excitement is visible among the vulture world when a procession is observed winding up the hill. From the summit a magnificent panorama of Bombay, with its harbour and the adjacent hills and islands, can be enjoyed. The Caves of Elephanta are situated on a wooded island about six miles from the city, and are very remarkable. They were built in honour of Brahminical deities, but the present Brahmins consider that the excavations and works are far too mighty to have been constructed by mortals. The most interesting is the Great Cave, in the form of a huge temple, at the far end of which, stands an immense three-faced bust, nineteen feet in height, representing Siva in three characters viz., as Brahma the Creator, Rudra the Destroyer, and Vishnu the Preserver; holding a lotus flower. Twenty-six colossal carved pillars support the roofs, but they have been much damaged. On entering the temple, on the right side is a small excavation containing a Lingain shrine which is worshipped on great occasions by thousands of Hindoos. Among other sights, worthy of note in Bombay are the town hall, which cost £60,000, the mint which before the closing of the mints to the free coinage of silver turned out 300,000 rupees daily, and the Victoria station of the Great Indian Peninsular Railway, which is one of the handsomest termini in the world, costing £30,000. It is a large building ornamented with sculptures and with a large central dome. The beautiful statue of Queen Victoria, by Noble, is of solid white marble and represents Her Majesty sitting on the throne. In front are the

Royal Arms and in the centre of the canopy is the Star of India, and above, the Rose of England, and Lotus of India, with the mottoes, "Dieu et Mon Droit," and "Heaven's light our Guide," in four languages. It cost 182,443 rupees, of which large sum 168,000 were given by H.H. the late Khanda Rao Gaekwar. Near to this is an equestrian bronze statue of the Prince of Wales, designed by Boehm, and presented to the city by Sir A. Sassoon.

Long railway journeys across the Continent of India must be made partly by night, and it is therefore necessary for travellers to provide themselves with sheets, a quilt and a pillow. The railway carriages are comfortable and there is not much vibration. Leaving Bombay from the Colaba station at nine o'clock p.m., on the 29th January, we commenced our long journey across India to

Calcutta, and arrived at the first stopping place, Ahmedebad, at ten the next morning. This once most beautiful city, contains 146,000 inhabitants, and is said at one time to have been the handsomest in Hindostan. It is surrounded by an ancient wall with twelve gateways and is full of mosques and temples mostly of the Jaina order of architecture. The population are Hindoos and Mahommedans and are occupied chiefly as goldsmiths, copper and brass workers. The principal mosque is called the Jumna Musjid, and was built by Sultan Ahmed I. in 1424. One enters a vast quadrangle on the west side of which is the mosque of white marble supported by 250 Jaina columns, exquisitely carved. In one corner is a raised balcony, enclosed with most elegantly traceried windows, in which the ladies of the harem are wont to attend service. Passing from this mosque we went on to that of the Queen of the Ahmed Shah, which is of white and black marble, finely carved. Just outside the Delhi gate is the magnificent Hindoo temple of Hattering, surmounted by 53 pagoda domes of pure Jaina style. It cost 1,000,000 rupees. This temple consists of an inner and outer chamber, both paved with coloured marbles ; in the latter is the god Dharnath who is represented as a beautiful youth. Mr. Ferguson, the great authority upon Indian Architecture, says :—

"Each part increases in dignity to the sanctuary. The exterior expresses the interior more completely than even a Gothic design, and whether looked at from its courts or from the outside it possesses variety without confusion, and an appropriateness of every part to the purpose intended."

Hundreds of small silver squirrels with beautifully marked fur were to be seen playing about on the sides of the mosques and houses. The present city, inside the walls, consists of large numbers of native houses, some of them with fine carved wood fronts, for which Ahmedebad is famous. At certain points in the streets there are resting places for birds, some of them brightly painted. Round these, parrots, crows, pigeons, etc., are to be seen, while kites and vultures are constantly wheeling in the air. The English cantonment lies about $3\frac{1}{2}$ miles out of the city, and on the road thither, one passes an avenue of trees, the haunt of thousands of parrots. On one of the houses in the city we noticed about twenty large sized monkeys; and on our purchasing some green ginger for them, they commenced to leap from one side of the street to another in a frenzy of excitement.

Ahmedebad is purely Oriental; droves of buffaloes, asses, goats, and camels, are to be seen coming in and out of the old city gates. Inside the wall one can scarcely proceed for the throngs of people in the streets. Mahommedans and Hindoos with their various coloured turbans, women wearing tawdry brass jewellery in their noses and silver bangles on their feet, attired in red striped cottons, but worn in graceful folds and carrying large brass water holders on their heads, or with their naked children carried astraddle on their hips, present an "ensemble" of colouring not easily forgotten.

January 27*th.*—Quitting Ahmedebad by the narrow gauge line, the train sped through an unattractive flat country, cultivated mostly with rice and maize, interspersed with patches of jungle and tracts of sand, upon which numbers of large sized grey and brown coloured monkeys were often noticed. In one place there must have been over one hundred sitting cosily together quite "en famille," and watching the train with great nonchalance. They would have charmed the children at home. The full grown animals had tails quite two feet long. Occasionally we observed, stately silver cranes stalking away, and handsome white and black feathered storks with long red beaks, and herons, by sides of ponds and watercourses. The plantations are all hedged with the prickly cactus which effectually keeps cattle in their own boundaries. The railway stations through this district of Rajpootana are built of red brick, surmounted by white-painted, mosquelike domes, upon which large numbers of pigeons congregate. Abu station is the junction for Mount Abu, a sanatorium for Europeans, situated 4,000 feet above us, to which one has to be conveyed by elephant. At this place are two of the most beautiful

Jaina temples in Hindostan, built in the 10th and 11th centuries. The more modern one was built by two brothers, and quoting Fergusson again, is "for minute delicacy of carving and beauty of detail, unrivalled in this country of patient labour." The scenery changes round this neighbourhood. Out of the dreary plain, brown and reddish-tinted precipitous mountains rose abruptly, while in place of tilled ground, stunted trees and low bushes were seen, under and around which large numbers of black buffaloes and grey coloured cattle found a scanty herbage. The only birds visible were black ringed doves, flying about or resting in pairs in the low trees. From Abu the line traversed a sandy wilderness until Ajmère was reached.

Ajmère is a city with a population of 67,000 and is very antique. There are two great objects of interest. The first is the Dargah, a mosque containing the tomb of Chisti, who is venerated both by Hindoos and Mahommedans alike. Woollen socks have to be put over one's boots on entering, and passing under a lofty gateway into a courtyard, one notices two large iron cauldrons known as the great and little "Deg." At the annual fair and pilgrimage, a rich pilgrim may give a "deg" feast. The smallest sum necessary to buy sufficient rice, butter, sugar, almonds, raisins and spice is 1,000 Rupees. When this huge rice pudding has been cooked, by means of a furnace placed beneath, it is scrambled for, boiling hot. When the cauldron is nearly emptied, the men of Indrakot tumble in together and scrape it clean. It is considered to be a miracle that no lives have been lost, though burns are frequent. Sometimes 20,000 pilgrims assemble at this festival. The tomb of the saint has a silver screen under a beautiful canopy, but we were not allowed to pass nearer than 20 yards. On the west side is a handsome mosque built of white marble, erected by the Mogul Emperor Shah Jehan, grandson of the Great Akbar. On leaving this sanctuary, wreaths of flowers were thrown round our necks with which we drove away to visit the celebrated mosque of Arkai-din-ka-jhompra, or the hut of two and a half days, which is so called from a legend that it was built in that time.

The glory of this mosque is the screen of seven arches, the centre one of which rises to a height of 56 feet, and Mr. Ferguson says of this, that—

"It is one of the most remarkable objects in India, and nothing can exceed the taste with which the Cufic and Togra inscriptions are interwoven with the more purely architectural decorations, or the manner in which they give life and variety to the whole, and nothing in Persia or Cairo is so exquisite in detail."

This ruined mosque lies in a hollow of the hills above the city. Leaving Ajmère, in a few hours we arrived in Jeypore, the principal charm of which is its varied life. The costumes worn by the people are most diversely coloured, as they are never twice alike and the women wear more silver bangles on their feet, more silver and brass jewellery in their noses and more bracelets on their arms, than in any other part of the country. The Mahommedan women, when travelling, wear white dresses covering the whole of their bodies with the exception of two eyeholes, and Hindoo women wear veils which they sometimes coquettishly draw aside, displaying a piercing eye and nut brown cheek. Jeypore has no mosques or temples of note, but in itself it is a study in rose, a romance of pink colouring.

One enters a quaint quadrangle and finds oneself surrounded by high towering walls all painted a delicate pink tint, relieved with frescoes of white flowers, then on through a noble gateway of the same colour, into a fine broad street, 111 feet wide and two miles in length. On both sides bazaars and houses of the same colour, stretching as far as the eye can reach, are cut at right angles by similar streets, and with noble open squares where thousands of pigeons are seen feeding; elephants with handsome coloured trappings and heads painted with quaint devices; camels carrying women and children as well as produce; white asses with loads of hay and wool; yokes of buffaloes with their horns painted blue and red, drawing small and curiously shaped carriages, covered with a red or blue tent arranged to protect inmates from the sun; small native carts by hundreds, all filled with natives of different castes, distinguished by their turbans; giving the "new arrival" in India an idea of being transported into the realities of the Arabian Nights. Everything in Jeypore centres round the Maharajah, his suite, his soldiers and fairy-like palaces. The palace and the gardens belonging to him cover one-seventh of the whole of the city. The retainers seemed to be having very easy times as they were sitting about in groups smoking very unconcernedly at the entrance of the palace. The Maharajah has 60 fighting elephants and 200 others. Proceeding through the old Palace we entered firstly, the Dewan-i-Khas or private hall of audience, built entirely of white marble, and then through a suite of rooms, with fine tiger skins, to a separate part of the gardens, where the modern palace stands, seven stories in height, painted a gaudy yellow, with white frescoes.

This is not shown to visitors, but the gardens and grounds were very beautiful and adorned with fine fountains. At the bottom is a lake where large numbers of turtles and alligators are to be seen. The menagerie is situated in a large park, one of the finest in India, 70 acres in extent, the most noteworthy animals being some fine man-eating tigers. In the centre of the park stands the Albert hall, a sumptuous modern building, the foundation stone of which was laid by H.R.H. the Prince of Wales, in 1876. It contains a large Durbar hall, with paintings of the Maharajahs and a Museum of Indian works of art and antiquities. Over the arches of the inner quadrangle, I noticed the following mottoes of Indian wisdom written both in English and Hindostani:

"Do nought to others which if done to thee would cause thee pain, this is the sum of duty."

" He has all wealth who has a mind contented."

" To one whose foot is covered with a shoe, the earth appears all carpeted with leather."

The most interesting excursion from Jeypore is to the ancient city, now called Ambère. After driving for a few miles past lovely gardens and temples and noticing splendid specimens of peacocks, (the sacred bird of India), the carriages stopped and three large elephants specially sent by his Highness the Maharajah were awaiting us. (One has to obtain an especial permission from the palace before proceeding.) Elephant riding may have terrors to many, but it really is not so bad. The sensation at first, is something like that of being on board ship in a gale, besides the fact of the wobbling motion shaking you up in all directions. However, we soon got used to the novelty, and after ascending a hill, at the top of which was a fortified gateway, we descended into a valley with wooded heights on both sides. Passing along the valley the palace soon came into view, in a most picturesque situation at the mouth of a rocky gorge, under which nestled a lovely lake. Our elephant carried us right into the great courtyard, where we dismounted and we were shown firstly a small temple, where a goat offered to the Hindoo god Kali preserves the tradition of a daily "human" sacrifice on the same spot in pre-historic times. The palace itself is situated on a higher terrace, and is literally an "enchanted palace of glass and marble." The entrance is a splendid gateway covered with mosaics and sculptures. We passed through this and noticed a small pavilion with latticed windows of alabaster. Then across a green garden surrounded by palaces, all of Jeypore mosaics, and with latticed marble windows.

The one on the left is called the Hall of Victory and is adorned with panels of carved alabaster and inlaid with flowers, while the roof glitters with the mirrored work for which Jeypore is renowned. Then followed bathing rooms of marble. Above this was the Jas Mandir Palace,—which is best described by Mr. Ferguson,—" Glowing with bright and tender colours and exquisite inlaid work, and looking through arches of carved alabaster, and clusters of slender columns upon the sleeping lake and the silent mountains."

Beneath us the ruined city was lying, while in the distance stretched a broad plain, bordered by ranges of mountains, over which ruins of the ancient walls and watch towers were to be seen.

February 1st.—We left Jeypore for the city of Delhi, and which is called the "Rome of Asia," because of the enormous extent of its ruins. Delhi is situated in a fertile plain, watered by the river Jumna. The sights are—the fort, the old palace, the Mahommedan mosque of Jumna Musjid, and the ridge of land outside the city gates celebrated in connection with the Indian mutiny. The fort forms part of the palace itself, and with its giant walls of red sandstone, is one of the most massive structures in the world. The British have committed a frightful act of vandalism in building an ugly barracks, (English pattern) in the centre of the palace grounds, and to do so they pulled down the whole of the harem courts. The palace covered twice the area of the Escurial, and measured 1,000 feet east and west by 3,200 feet north and south. The most beautiful portion remaining is called the Dewan-i-Khas or private Audience Hall. It is of pure white marble inlaid with precious stones and is in the form of an open hall, built of beautiful arches of the carved Hindoo pattern, and with four domes at the corners. Round the roof runs the following inscription;—

"If there is a heaven on earth, it is this, it is this, none but this."

The whole fort is surrounded by a noble red wall with towers and kiosks at intervals. The entrance hall is described in "Indian Architecture," as being "375 feet in length; has very much the effect of a gigantic Gothic cathedral and forms the noblest entrance known as belonging to any existing palace."

The Mosque of Jumna Musjid stands on an elevated plateau in the centre of the city, and is of red sandstone with white marble domes, and unrivalled for its size. In it we were shown the following relics of Mahomet: a footprint in marble; a slipper, and also copies of the Koran by the nephew of Mahomet. Five thousand workmen were employed for six years in building this mosque.

At the top of the ridge outside the city walls a handsome Gothic shaped tower, in commemoration of the mutiny has been erected, and bears the names of the regiments and batteries who served, and of the officers who died, in the performance of their duty. In the plain to the north is the spot where Her Majesty the Queen was proclaimed Empress of India on the 1st January 1877, by Lord Lytton, in presence of all the great princes and chiefs of India, and an army of about 50,000 men. The city of Delhi, apart from the above-mentioned sights, and its historical interest for Englishmen, is not so interesting as Jeypore. The streets seemed dirty and ill-kept and its bazaars are small and insignificant. The whole place is infested with touts, who pester one's existence with all kinds of cheap armour and embroideries.

About 11 miles across the plain, which is covered with ancient tombs, the old city of Delhi is situated. The remains of the Kutub mosque are the most beautiful in India. The walls are of Mahommedan architecture, covered with most ornate carving in Arabic characters and flowered tracery; the pillars are of pure Jaina style and the whole pile is a most majestic ruin. The arches are very beautifully carved and are well preserved. In the central quadrangle stands an iron column, 23 feet in height, one of the curiosities of India, with an inscription upon it of the fourth century. Mr. Ferguson says of it,—" Taking A.D. 400 as a mean date, it opens our eyes to a state of affairs to find the Hindoos of that age capable of forging a bar of iron longer than any that have been found in Europe up to a very late date. It is almost equally startling to find that after an exposure to wind and rain for fourteen centuries, it is unrusted, and that the capitol and inscriptions are as clear and as sharp now as when put up." Close to these ruins stands the minaret of the Kutub Minar, 245 feet in height, which looks really what it was intended to be, a "tower of victory."

February 4th.—Leaving Delhi by the East Indian Railway, we cross the River Jumna by a handsome girder bridge of 12 spans, each of 205 feet, and in six hours we see before us the dome of the white marble tomb of the Taj Mahal, situated on the banks of the above-mentioned river, and just outside the city of Agra. On the left side, as we approach over the bridge, rises the huge crenellated masonry of the walls of the fort, enclosing the remains of the palace, over which the Union Jack is flying. Agra is famed for its gold and silver embroideries, carving in soap stone and inlaid work,—called pietra dura,—in white marble. The population is about 165,000 and essentially Mahommedan. The great builders here were Akbar who reigned from 1556 to 1605, and his grandson Shah Jehan. Their styles of buildings were very different, the one showing a vigorous, manly style, and the other ornamental prettiness; but both have left marvels of architecture that are unrivalled in the world. Firstly, I must mention the palace, enclosed in the citadel, built entirely of red sand stone, with Indian sculptures. The whole palace is one-and-half miles in circumference and is built on the banks of the Jumna. Shah Jehan added to this colossal building several wings all of white marble, elegantly carved. The Pearl mosque is a perfect gem. In the centre of the palace is a great court, 500 feet by 370 feet, approached by a succession of beautiful courts. At the side is the great Hall of the Palace, the Dewanni Aum, all of white marble with three ranges of Moorish arcades. Behind these are smaller courts, one containing the private hall of audience and the other the harem. Near to this stands a beautiful marble pavilion, inlaid with precious stones, from which a beautiful panorama of the country and the Taj Mahal can be seen.

Leaving this palace by the massive Delhi gate we visited the Jumna Musjid mosque, noted for its three great domes without necks, like inverted balloons, and built of red sandstone, with band of white marble.

From these we drove out to pay our first visit to the glorious Taj Mahal, or the Crown Lady's tomb, built by Shah Jehan for his wife the beautiful Princess Nour Mahal. This is the most celebrated mausoleum in the world, and without doubt it is the show thing of Northern India. It is of great size and took seventeen years to build, many thousands of men being employed. Passing through a noble gateway of red sandstone, in itself a work of art, ornamented with inscriptions from the Koran, and surmounted by 26 cupolas, we enter a beautiful Indian garden, filled with rare shrubs, cypresses and flowering trees, at the end of which, on a large white marble plateau, stood the tomb, all of white marble, inlaid with pietra dura work and surmounted by a handsome dome. At the four corners of the platform were four marble minarets, each 133 feet high. In the interior where the show tombs are, says Mr. Ferguson :—

"The light is admitted only through double screens of white marble trellis work of the most exquisite design. No words can describe the chastened beauty of that central chamber, seen in the soft gloom of the subdued light. When used as a pleasure palace, it must always have been the coolest and loveliest of retreats, and now that it is sacred to the dead, it is the most graceful and the most impressive of sepulchres in the world."

We visited the Taj again by moonlight and then the effect is almost indescribable.

Twenty three miles from Agra is situated the deserted city and palace of Fatepor Sikri, reached only by a carriage road lined with trees the whole way, which give a pleasant shade to what might be otherwise a hot and dusty drive. The chief glory of the palace which was built by the great Akbar, is the mosque, which is a copy of the one at Mecca. It measures 550 feet by 470 feet and is surmounted by three domes. In its large quadrangle stands the tomb of Selim Chisti (a Mahommedan saint), of white marble with the most intricate lattice work screens. The doors are of solid ebony, ornamented with brass. Over the tomb itself is a large canopy of mother of pearl. Both Hindoos and Mahommedans resort to this tomb and pray to the saint to intercede in their favour. The gateway of the mosque towers to a height of 130 feet and is one of the noblest in India. The walls are 80 feet high. On one side is a large tank filled with water to the depth of 30 feet, and two men gave us an exhibition of diving from this fearful height into the tank below.

The palace itself stands on a sandstone ridge, and the most celebrated portions worth mentioning here, are three richly sculptured pavilions, built for the monarch's three favourite Sultanas; viz., his Hindoo wife, Bir Bul Ka Beti, the daughter of his favourite minister, Bir Bul; Minain's house and the palace of the Roumi Sultana.

About nine miles from the city, at Secundara, is the gigantic pyramidal tomb of Akbar, standing in an extensive garden, approached by a handsome gateway, inlaid with marble. In the centre of a garden rise four terraces from an elevated platform, 30 feet high and measuring 320 feet each way. On the summit of the highest terrace surrounded by a colonnade of marble, is the mausoleum, but the real burial place is in a vaulted chamber in the basement, exactly under the simulated tomb on the summit. Mr. Ferguson says :—

"That no such royal tomb as this remains exposed to the air in any Indian Mausoleum."

The following extract from "Indian Architecture," by Mr. Ferguson, D.C.L., F.R.S., M.R.A.S., upon the subject of Indian tombs, is worth reading :—

"The princes of the Tartar races in carrying on their love of tombs, made it the practice to build their own in their lifetimes, as all people must who are desirous of sepulchral magnificence. They build their sepulchres of such a character as to serve for places of enjoyment for themselves and their friends during lifetime, and only when they could enjoy them no longer they became the solemn resting places of their mortal remains. The usual process for the erection of these structures is for the king or noble who intends to provide himself a tomb, to enclose a garden outside the city walls, generally with high castellated walls and with one or more splendid gateways; and in the centre of this he erects a square or octagonal building crowned by a dome, and in the more splendid examples with smaller and dome roofed apartments on four of the sides, the other four being devoted to entrances. This building is generally situated on a lofty square terrace, from which radiate four broad alleys, generally with marble paved canals, ornamented with fountains; the angular spaces are planted with cypresses and other evergreens and fruit trees, making up one of those formal but characteristic gardens so common in the East. During the lifetime of the founder, the central building is called a Bairah Durrie, or festal hall, and is used as a place of recreation and feasting by him and his friends. At his death its destination is changed; the founder's remains are interred beneath the central dome. Sometimes his favourite wife lies besides him; but more generally his family and relations are buried beneath the collateral domes. When once used as a place of burial, its vaults never again resound with festal mirth. The care of the building is handed over to priests and cadis, who gain a scanty subsistence by the sale of the fruit of the garden, or the alms of those who come to visit the last resting place of their friend or master. Perfect silence takes the place of festivity and mirth. The beauty of the surrounding objects combine with the repose of the place to produce an effect as graceful as it is solemn and appropriate. Though these tombs, with the remains of their enclosures, are so numerous throughout all India, the Taj Mahal, at Agra, is almost the only tomb that retains its garden in anything like its pristine beauty; and there is not perhaps in the whole world, a scene where nature and art so successfully combine to produce a perfect work of art as within the precincts of this far famed Mausoleum."

One other tomb must be mentioned, viz.: that of Itimadu Daulah, because it is one of the finest buildings in Agra. This mausoleum is encased with white marble and inlaid with the pietra dura work. There are four octagonal towers at each corner and in the centre a raised pavilion, in which are the two yellow marble sarcophagi of Ghayas Beg (who was prime minister to Jehangis, 1605) and his wife. On each side of the entrance is beautiful marble lattice work. There are seven other minor tombs and the whole effect is very lovely.

CHAPTER IV.

Indian Bird Life—Hindoo Marriage—Native Bazaar in Agra — Cawnpore — Sites of the Massacre — Memorial Well — Lucknow — The Residency — The Great Imambarah—Benares—The Monkey Temple — Cremation — Bathing in Ganges— Calcutta — River Hooghly.

IN India, bird life is interesting, partly because the Hindoos hold them in great reverence. In most of the cities we have visited, feeding places are provided for them, and even in villages wooden trays are hung out under the trees, where one may see crows, pigeons, doves, paroquets, etc., congregated. In Jeypore and in Agra this bird life was very noticeable. Literally thousands of pigeons filled the squares and market squares of the former city, and in the air one sees kites and vultures flying and often swooping down and resting upon the housetops. Then the crow; well he is everywhere and a far different specimen to his English coadjutor in villainy. Instead of remaining in his congenial fields, he descends upon country towns and villages, caws cheekily at you from every housetop, gets in your way at railway stations, under your horse's legs, makes off impudently with children's breakfasts and in fact laughs humanity to scorn. The trees and streets are full of them all day, and when dusk sets in they return to the country to roost, coming back, as it were, to business in the morning. Walking about five o'clock along a country road outside Jeypore, thousands were seen coming from the city, accompanied by paroquets in small parties of four or five, emitting small shrieks as they flew past. In spite of this unpleasant note, however, they are great favourites, because of their bright green plumage and on account of the novelty of seeing so many in a wild state. The cream coloured doves with black rings round their necks utter their soft cooing notes everywhere. The most beautiful bird of all, is of course, the peacock, called "the sacred bird of India," and in the suburbs of Jeypore, among the picturesque ruined tombs and gardens, the peacock with a luxuriant and glossy plumage, unsurpassed anywhere, looks his best. The jay is very common and looks picturesque with his beautiful blue wings, flying across the fields. Another black bird of the starling tribe, called a minar, with a red beak and white wings is seen very often, also a quaint woodpecker, striped black and white,—zebra fashion,—with a large brown comb on his head and a beak an inch long. The most noticeable, perhaps, of all is the sives, a bird nearly six feet high, with a beak a foot in length and legs nearly three feet long and looking most solemnly and sedately at you. One hardly knows how to take this bird, whether, if you proceed, he will give way first, or, open his long beak and make for you.

February 4th.—We met a Hindoo wedding procession this afternoon, passing through a wood. It was headed by a man riding a white donkey and carrying a flag, then came a band, the members of which were dressed in scarlet, and large sized models of elephants borne on wheels and resplendent with gold and silver tinsel. Then came the youthful bridegroom about six years old carried in a covered litter, followed by numbers of friends in picturesque yecca carts, four live elephants with coloured howdahs from which large bells were suspended;—the animals' heads being painted with the religious sectarial mark; women and men carrying presents of bread on their heads. The whole procession was accompanied by plenty of the discordant tom-toming for which the Hindoos have such a liking.

Shopping in the native bazaar in Agra is a pleasant occupation. Beautifully worked silver and gold embroidered slippers, the Indian narghili pipes, brass work and handsome embroideries are the staple commodities. We visited also some sculpture works where the "pietra dura" inlay work is carried on and were shown a magnificent model of the Taj destined for the Chicago exhibition, which had taken two-and-a-half years to complete. The price asked was 1,500 rupees, but as the Americans now levy a duty of

62% upon objects of fine art, the figure asked in Chicago will be very much higher.

February 6th.—Proceeding by rail from Agra we arrived at the city of Cawnpore in seven-and-a-half hours. Cawnpore has no mosques, temples, tombs, or palaces of note; its only interest for the stranger centering in and around the sites made famous by the fearful massacres of the Indian Mutiny. The place is therefore classic ground for the Briton; and the Government and the English relations and friends of those slaughtered by the cruelty of Nana Sahib, have placed on the different hallowed spots suitable monuments and memorials. The first we visited was a small garden enclosed with iron palisading in the centre of which stood an Ionic cross bearing the following inscription :—

"In a well under this cross, were laid by yᵉ hands of yᵉ fellows in suffering yᵉ bodies of men, women and children, who died hard during ye heroic defence of Wheeler's Entrenchment, when beleaguered by ye rebel Nana, June 1857."

Near to this, bounded by a dwarf green hedge, was the square entrenchment ground which Wheeler so gallantly defended with about 300 soldiers against 3,000 well trained and well fed native soldiers for 21 days. The total number of women, children and civilians in the entrenchment was about 1,000, and as the earthworks were only about four feet high, one can easily imagine the perilous position in which the Europeans were placed. In less than three weeks 250 succumbed and were buried in the well just mentioned. In one corner of this enclosed ground still stands the well, riddled with shot, from which women and children fetched water for the use of the gallant defenders.

The following brief historical account of the massacre one may well recall to memory:—

"On the 26th, there was an armistice and it was mutually agreed, that upon the British surrendering their position, their guns and treasure, that they would have safe conduct to the riverside and that boats would be provided by Nana Sahib to take them down the Ganges. It was about nine o'clock when all were embarked, and then, upon the sounding of a bugle, the native boatmen clambered out of the boats and a murderous fire of grapeshot and musketry opened upon the wretched passengers who had thus been brought to the shambles. The thatch of the boats took fire and the sick and wounded were burnt, while the Sepoys jumped into the water and butchered the rest. Orders then came from Nana to kill no more women, and about 125 women wounded and half drowned were then carried back to Cawnpore. One boat drifted down the river. Those on board propelled it as they could, but their numbers were rapidly diminished by the fire from the banks. For 36 hours they floated down stream, pursued and attacked by the enemy on all sides. On the second morning they awoke to find themselves in a side stream with Sepoys on the banks ready to overwhelm them. The 11 soldiers who alone remained, gallantly leapt on shore, led by two officers, and dispersed the astounded crowd, but the boat had drifted down stream and was lost to them. Four of these men, Mowbray Thompson, Delafosse, Privates Murphy and Sullivan, being strong swimmers reached the Oudh shore, and alone lived to tell the story of Cawnpore. The boat was subsequently overtaken by the enemy and 80 people were brought back. The men were then all shot by order of the Nana, and the women and children sent to the Savada to join the 125, whom for his own purposes, Nana had rescued from the Massacre Ghat. These were afterwards removed to a small place called Bibi-garb, where between 7th and 14th July, 28 died. But retribution was at hand. On 7th July, General Havelock marched from Allahabad with 1,000 British soldiers, 130 Sikhs, 6 guns and 18 volunteer troopers. On the 12th, at 7 a.m. they halted at Belindah, four miles from Fatehpur. Here they were attacked by the

Nana's army, but it suffered a crushing defeat, and Fatehpur, where great atrocities had been committed by the rebels, was sacked by Havelock's men. On the 15th, Havelock again defeated the rebels and drove them over the bridge across the Pandemadi. The Nana was living riotously in a palace over the prison, and learning that Havelock was advancing upon him, issued an order to massacre the women and children in the Bibi-garb. The few men among the prisoners were brought out and killed in his presence. A party of Sepoys were then ordered to shoot the women, but they intentionally missed their aim. Then a party of butchers were sent in with swords and long knives. Soon the shrieks ceased, but the groans continued all through the night. In the morning the dead and dying, and a few children almost unhurt, were pitched into an adjoining well."

Adjoining the enclosure, is the Memorial Church, built in the Romanesque style at a cost of £20,000. The interior is very fine, the coloured marble pavement having been presented by the Maharajah of Jodhpor. All round the church are suitable tablets and memorial stones. From the church we drove down to the banks of the Ganges, which is about one mile broad, and crossed by the fine bridge of the Oudh railway, about one mile away, and arrived at the famous Massacre Ghat or steps. The melancholy spot is appropriately marked by a small simple cross, with the inscription "June, 1857." Close to it are the remains of a Hindoo temple dedicated to Siva, but now in ruins. From this spot we drove to the Memorial-Well and Gardens, which cover thirty acres and are beautifully laid out. On the spot over the fatal well, containing the bodies of 200 victims, is a Gothic, octagonally-shaped screen, and in the centre of this, is a beautiful white marble figure of the "Angel of the Resurrection," by Marochetti, with arms crossed on her breast. Round the wall the following words are placed :—

"Sacred to the perpetual memory of a great number of Christian people, chiefly women and children, who near this spot were cruelly murdered by the followers of the rebel Nana Dhandu Pant, of Bithur, and cast, the dying with the dead, into the well below, on the 15th day of July, 1857."

The gardens could not be laid out in better taste. Beautiful cypresses surround the the well, which is on a slight elevation, and on one side are two young cypress trees planted by the late lamented Duke of Clarence, when he visited Cawnpore. The city itself contains a population of 182,000, It is a great emporium of harness, shoes and leather work.

In three hours after leaving Cawnpore, we arrived in Lucknow, the fourth largest city in our Indian Empire, with a population of 272,600, three-fifths of which consists of Hindoos. Lucknow was "*en fête*," for it was the first day of the spring meeting of the local race-club. Going out to the grand stand about three miles away, we passed many handsome bungalows with well laid out gardens and grounds, beautifully timbered, and through broad fine avenues of tamarind trees. As the hotels were very full, the hospitable Englishmen had put large numbers of tents for the reception of guests from different parts of India. At the race-course, which reminded one of a small English club ground,* a military band was playing and about 1,000 people were in the enclosure, the most noticeable being a few Indian rajahs, arrayed in English tweed suits, but with characteristic coloured turbans, denoting their

---

* Like Sandown Park.

several castes. Outside the ring a small number of English soldiers with white helmets and a contingent of natives made up the company assembled. The racing was deadly dull, and the music was the most enjoyable part.

The inevitable American globe-trotter has not much consolation in visiting either Lucknow or Cawnpore. The historical interest attaching to both places he does not care about; a few hours are sufficient to obtain a cursory idea of what the cities are, and then he is off to Agra, Delhi, or Benares. But in Lucknow there is much to interest the intelligent tourist.* The first place to visit is the Residency, with the adjoining out-buildings, which are left in the same ruined state as they were after the memorable siege. They are surrounded by gardens,

---

* The city is very scattered, being seven miles across, and lies on the both banks of the river Goomti.

in which the lovely golden blossoms of the *Aristologia* are seen to perfection. Everyone remembers the gallant defence of Lucknow by Sir Henry Lawrence, who lost his life. Close to the Residency, from the ruined towers of which we obtained a good view of the surrounding country, is an artificial mound, with a handsome white marble monument, 20 feet high, on the summit. This is the Lawrence memorial, and on it is inscribed:—

In Memory of

MAJOR GEN. SIR HENRY LAWRENCE,

K.C.B.

And the brave men who fell
In defence of the Residency,

1857.

Near this is the Cemetery, where 2,000 men and women lie. A plain slab of white marble marks the spot where Henry Lawrence lies buried 'and on it are inscribed the following touching words, dictated by himself.

Here Lies

HENRY LAWRENCE,

Who tried to do his duty.

"May the Lord have mercy on his soul!"

Born 28th June, 1806,

Died 4th July, 1857.

The palace of the Kaiser Bagh next claimed our attention. This large building is built entirely of stucco, painted a bright yellow, and has no architectural merit whatever. It is arranged in the form of a large square, the centre of which is now planted with grass and in the open space the fair used to be held every August; all the inhabitants of the city being admitted. The most noteworthy buildings of all, however, are the Emambarah palace and mosque, where Asafadaulah lies buried.

The central or great hall is 163 feet long and 53 feet broad. A plain masonry slab marks where the king was interred. This palace was built in 1784, the year of the great famine, to afford relief to the people. Other buildings are the Husainabad Imanbarah, containing the throne of the king covered with beaten silver, and his wife's divan.

There is a quaint native bazaar, and the staple industry of the place is chased silver made from the rupee. The Indian Government evidently allow the coins to be melted down, because the silver is offered freely in the open bazaar, and one sees large numbers of money changers weighing quantities of rupees and disposing of them to the manufacturers. Lucknow is a very clean city and we are loth to leave, as our hotel, the Imperial, has afforded us the best apartments and food we have yet obtained in India; and we have Benares before us, which in spite of its being the holy city and containing some 2,000 temples, has a bad reputation in the way of smells and dirt, which is not inviting. The mail trains start at unearthly hours in India and we leave to-morrow February 10th, at 6.15 a.m. and hope to arrive at our destination 1.15 p.m.

February 10*th*.—Benares contains a large population of about 220,000, and it has been the religious capital of India from beyond historical times. It is certain that it was a flourishing place six years before the Christian era, for Sakya Muni, or Gautama, the founder of the Buddhist religion came to it from Gaya, as it was such an important centre, and he was born in 638 B.C.

To my surprise there is a clean as well as a dirty Benares, and our hotel is fortunately in the former, surrounded by charming gardens with fine trees. Broad roads also intersect this portion of the city. The old city is about three miles distant, so we drive off in a carriage with native servants dressed in picturésque turbans, to pay our first visit to it.

Our guide book tells us, that in the temple of Durga, commonly called the "monkey temple" by Europeans, *myriads* of monkeys are to be seen which inhabit the large trees near it. We found the temple to be a dirty building stained with red ochre, at the entrance to which was a band room where priests beat a large drum three times a day. We entered and found the usual open quadrangle with the temple of red sandstone in the centre, round which were about thirty monkeys, one goat, and two dogs; and several children offering trays of bread, etc., to feed the monkeys with. Durga is the terrific form of Siva's wife, who delights in sacrifice; goats are offered to her and we were shown the place where the sacrifices *sometimes* take place. At the entrance several hideous grinning monstrosities, as well as the priests, demanded the usual "backsheesh." We then visited a holy father, a really charming old ascetic, living by himself in *puris naturalibus* in a large garden. Dressed in a white cloak he came to receive us. He had been there for thirty years and was very learned in Sanscrit. He gave us a copy of the book and other writings, and showed us a marble idol of himself, in a small temple, presented to him by a neighbouring Maharajah, which bore a certain resemblance to the old man. The Earl and Countess Brownlow had visited him the previous day. With the aid of our guide we had a pleasant conversation with him; he expressed himself as sorry to lose us, shook us cordially with both hands and to our surprise, would accept nothing even for the poor; but a Nemesis awaited us outside, in the shape of ugly clamorous beggars.

Taking a barge on the Ganges we came to one of the sights of India, viz., the cremation of Hindoos on the banks of their sacred river. Large quantities of wood were stacked near the cremation ground, and three bodies draped in red and white were placed with their feet in the river, while the pyres were being prepared. The body of a Hindoo lady of a higher caste was floating on a bier in the water, and was covered with flowers and palm leaves. It is the melancholy duty of the nearest surviving relative, after the body has been placed on the wood and then covered over with more, to light the pyre. The fire must be brought from the house of a Domra, who is a man of the lowest caste. The instance before us was very pitiful. A poor old man went slowly to the Domra's house, brought the burning hay, with which he set fire to the wood, and as the flames ascended round the body, went up the steep bank of the river, weeping bitterly. The Hindoos are so superstitious that, unless the fire can be brought from the house of a Domra, they prefer to throw the bodies of their dead into the river. Close by, in a large house, a wedding was being celebrated with singing, dancing and music, while within 25 yards the earthly remains of three human beings were being burned. The ashes, etc., are thrown into the river. Landing shortly afterwards, we ascended one of the lofty minarets (150 feet) of Aurangzib's mosque, from which we enjoyed a picturesque bird's-eye view of the city immediately beneath us. This mosque was built as an insult to the Hindoos, by the Emperor Aurangzib, in the midst of their most sacred temples, over which it towers contemptuously.

The bazaars and streets in Benares in the neighbourhood of the temples are very narrow, and always inconveniently crowded with pilgrims who have come thousands of miles to bathe in the sacred waters of the Ganges; when therefore one of the numerous marriage processions passes, the scene is very brilliant. This morning (February 11th) we witnessed a procession, which obstructed the traffic in the narrow lane. The bridegroom was dressed in handsome gold brocade, with his face newly painted, and was preceded by caparisoned horses, carrying other young boys beautifully dressed, and wearing silver and gold ornaments, while silver bangles were worn by the horses. Bands accompanied the bridegroom, as well as all his relations and friends.

A Hindoo temple is never very large, and only interesting to Europeans on account of its architecture and carving. Most of the larger ones consist of two courts, an outer one open to the sky, and an inner building standing by itself in the quadrangle, which is the holy of holies, and contains the image of the particular deity to which the temple is dedicated. This inner sanctuary is too sacred for Christians to enter. It is strange that in Benares there are no temples dedicated to Brahma the creator, or Vishnu the destroyer, but to malignant deities like Siva and Durga. Benares is as much the stronghold of heathenism as Rome is of Roman-catholicism or Mecca of Mahommedanism, and missionaries cannot seem to storm it, because of the caste system. If once this goes, English missions, or more probably Roman-catholicism, because of its ornate ritual, would have a chance. This latter religion is already making great progress in Ceylon.

Hindoo worship has many peculiarities, but one that we cannot have much sympathy with is its dirtiness. Among the most holy shrines in Benares, to which pilgrims resort, is the Golden temple. This is a small red sandstone building, exquisitely carved and with three towers, two of which are covered with plates of gold over copper. The interior was crowded with pilgrims offering water and flowers to Siva. The floor was one mass of filth. Up and down the narrow lane came the throngs of people, some of them making offerings in the temple of Annapurna, meaning Anna, "food," and purna, "who filleth." This goddess is supposed to have special orders to feed the people of Benares. In her temple half a dozen sacred bulls were wandering at large, which added to the dirtiness, and the stench of the decaying flowers was indescribable. If the goddess feeds the people, at all events the beggars outside came off badly, and one of her priests followed us for a mile for further gratuities. There are four shrines in this temple, dedicated to the Sun, Ganesh, Gauri Shanker, and the Monkey god Hanuman. In the street close by is the strange figure of the god Ganesh, squatting on a stone. This ugly idol is represented with a huge red face, with an elephant's trunk in lieu of nose, and silver hands, feet and ears. As the

Hindoos esteem ugliness this idol is continually receiving offerings of water and flowers. The sight, however, of Benares is the bathing of thousands of men and women from the fifty ghāts or flights of stone steps, which descend from the most famous buildings to the river. The best manner to see this, is to hire a barge and be rowed along the banks. Aged, ascetic, holy men, fakirs, portly Bráhman priests, Madrassie men and women, priests and children attend in many coloured gowns, while sacred bulls, pariah dogs, and horrible beggars are also to be seen. The most sacred of all the ghāts is the Manikaranika, and here were multitudes jostling one another in the desire to reach the water's edge. Near this ghāt is a well which is also worshipped. Offerings of milk, sandal wood, sweetmeats and water are thrown into it and from the putrefaction of these a stench arises that would have frightened the witch of Endor herself. The cow ghāt is also uncommon from a stone figure of a cow there, and because of the large numbers of cows which frequent it.

At the Panchanga ghāt the Hindoos have a superstition that five rivers meet, but one sees only the Ganges, and has to imagine the other four. At Allahabad there is also a superstition that three rivers meet. There are only two visible, the Ganges and the Jumna, but the faithful imagine a third. A story is told of a rajah who died in Italy, and after some difficulty, permission was obtained for his cremation, but it was necessary for the body to be cremated at the junction of three rivers, and as there was no such junction in the country, they burnt the body at the confluence of two, and imagined a third, and all went well with the departed rajah.

In addition to the bathers, there are

numbers of women carrying brass bowls on their heads, ascending and descending the steps to fetch the Ganges water, which they drink. After bathing, the people always wash the gowns which they have worn at the river side. It seems a most suitable religion for this climate, that enforces bathing upon the Hindoos before eating, or they would assuredly not do so. Hundreds of small temples line the banks containing idols. With the exception of the palace and buildings on the river banks, there are no other buildings of note in Benares. On the south side is a fine steel bridge of the Oudh and Rohilkand Railway, 12,000 yards long; this we crossed on our journey to Calcutta, which occupied $16\frac{1}{2}$ hours.

February 12th.—We have only two days to spend in this city, as our berths are booked for Burmah for the 14th inst. Calcutta, however, offers no charms to the traveller in the Orient, as the city is quite European in style. Chowringee is the fashionable quarter, and here there are large numbers of stately boarding houses and private palaces, which have been the cause of the place receiving the title of a City of Palaces. There is a population of 840,000, and the city, which is the capital of the Bengal Presidency, lies on the banks of the river Hooghly, a branch of the Ganges. The sights are few and can be quickly enumerated. The Presidency is a fine building erected in 1804 and is surrounded by extensive gardens. The most noticeable public building is the post office, which has a handsome dome. Near this is the site of the famous Black Hole. The Eden gardens form a pleasant lounge and are illuminated by the electric light at night. In the centre is an elaborately carved Hindoo pagoda. A breezy expanse of common is called the

Maidan, upon which fine monuments are erected, the largest of which is the Ochterlony monument, in honour of Sir David Ochterlony. This is a fine obelisk, from the summit of which a bird's eye view of the city is to be obtained. There are equestrian statutes to Lord Mayo, and Sir James Outram, as well as standing figures in marble of Lords W. Bentinck, Northbrook, Canning, Lawrence, and Hardinge. Calcutta possesses the largest pontoon bridge in the world—1,500 feet long. The river Hooghly is very picturesque with its forests of masts, and were it not for the clear blue sky overhead, is not unlike the Thames.

The hotels in India are execrable and the food worse. There is not one really good hotel from Bombay to Calcutta. The reason for this is given in the hospitality of the English resident, who receives all Britons armed with letters of introduction into his bungalow. But now things are changed. There is an enormous influx of globe trotters, mostly Americans and Australians, but very few English, crossing India on their way round the world, and instant reform is necessary. The present hotels are mostly kept by natives, who have no idea of modern sanitation or comfort, and the accommodation is perfectly piggish.

We are now leaving for Burmah on board the British India Steamship, " Goa," of 1900 tons and are sailing pleasantly down the river Hooghly, the banks of which are quite Bengalese with their low fringes of palms, under which native huts are seen occasionally, while beyond, mango groves and rice fields are to be seen.

Our impressions of India have been very pleasant. The people seem now to be prosperous, happy, and contented under British rule. We have given the country railways and education, and the cities are becoming modernised, while the magnificent remains of the glorious tombs, temples, and palaces, are being looked after by Government and kept from further decay. The modern suburbs and towns are laid out on a princely scale, as there is no scarcity of land. Boulevards of stately trees line the principal streets, and afford shelter from the sun.

As I write, the river is broadening, the shores of Bengal are fading from view, and so we bid farewell to Hindostan.

CHAPTER V.

Burmah—Mandalay — The Mingoon Bell — River Irrawaddy — Pagán — Prome — Rangoon — The Golden Pagoda — S.S. Pentakota — Moulmein — Penang—Singapore.

THE distance from Calcutta to Rangoon, the capital of Lower Burmah, is 787 miles. It is fortunate that we are travelling across the sea of Bengal during the month of February, because the cyclones, which are frequent in these seas, have never been known to occur during this month. After a three days' quiet sail we awoke early on Friday morning to find ourselves in the Rangoon river in a dense fog. About nine o'clock it lifted and Rangoon itself was visible, with its beautiful Golden Pagoda glittering in the fierce sunlight. The river was crowded with shipping, while long processions of the fish-shaped paddy boats, conveying rice up and down stream, with their square shaped sails and the sampan bird canoe, painted red, white and blue, were also to be seen. Soon after arrival at Rangoon, we took train for Mandalay, the capital of Upper Burmah, and the former residence of the dethroned King Theebaw. The line passed through wild jungle and miles of picturesque teak forests. The site of Mandalay is very beautiful, lying as it does in an open plain, watered by the river Irrawaddy. We reached the city in 23 hours and found it to be a veritable city of dust. All the trees were covered with white dust, resembling a hoar frost, while the roads were inches deep with it. There are 184,000 inhabitants. The remains of the palace, which was partially destroyed, are of ornamental carved wood, highly gilded and stained, situated in a large walled enclosure nearly square, a mile and a half in circumference. Outside this wall is a broad moat of water running round the four sides, in which lotus flowers were growing. Just above the city rises Mandalay hill, and on its summit is a wooden shrine of Buddha to which pilgrimages are made. Immediately beneath lies the city with its countless pagodas, the fertile plain covered with rice fields, through which the broad waters of the Irrawaddy run, and the distant mountains. About two miles away is the pagoda of Aracan, containing one of the first images of Buddha that was brought from India over the Aracan hills. It stands in a chapel decorated with precious stones, and is a barbaric study in gold. Offerings of gold leaf are made to this shrine, and pilgrims can see these offerings being added to the image. There are now about four inches of gold on the figure which is becoming larger and larger. Near to this were the ruined temple and pagoda of the city of Anapura containing hundreds of marble Buddhas, from baby size to colossal giants, covered with gold and glittering gems.

In the centre of Mandalay rises the bell-shaped Golden Pagoda from a paved courtyard planted with tamarind trees, under whose shelter pretty little Burmese girls were playing and offering lovely lotus flowers, while old hags were smoking their dirty green leaf cigars, even in Buddha's holy of holies.

About six miles up the river at a place called Mingoon is the colossal bell. It was cast on the other side of the river by king Mingoon, Theebaw's predecessor and is said to be the second largest bell in the world, the largest being the one at Moscow. It weighs 90 tons. Close to it is an ugly square brick structure of enormous size, which was also commenced by the king, with the idea of building a king's pagoda. Near it is the queen's pagoda containing hundreds of white marble images of Buddha, each two feet high.

The Burmese are all Buddhists and are happy in having no caste prejudices, and can intermarry where they like. In fact their marriage laws are extremely lax; the only ceremony necessary when a couple desire to dissolve partnership is to shut themselves up in a hut, illumine two candles, and the owner of the one first extinguished walks away, leaving the remaining "he" or "she" in peaceable possession. The men are very strong and are tattooed all over their backs, while the women have expressive faces with coquettish manners, and dress like the Japanese. They are, however, very indolent and are called the Irish of the East, being fond of an idle life, while the women and even children smoke long cigars made of the green tobacco leaf, filled with green tobacco and pieces of wood.

The Buddhist priests are called phoongyes, and are not supposed to eat after mid-day, and then only what is presented to them by the natives. They are attired in bright yellow flowing silk gowns and carry large fans made of palm leaf to protect their heads, which are clean shaved, from the sun. The younger priests also carry brass ewers to receive the food offerings. Many houses are built on piles, about ten feet from the ground, to protect the inhabitants from miasma.

Leaving Mandalay, on Tuesday the 21st February, we embarked on board the Irrawaddy Flotilla Company's steamer "China," for a trip down the river to Prome, nearly 800 miles distant. The Irrawaddy is 1,400 miles long and is supposed to be the fourth largest river in the world. The vessels are built especially for the traffic, drawing only four-and-a-half feet of water and are 300 feet in length, of 1,000 tons, and are capable of carrying on the twin decks no fewer than 2,000 passengers. In addition to this, large convoys of "flats" as they are termed, are roped on to the side of the vessel, and hold natives, horses, cattle, provender, &c. Both of these are protected from the sun by roofs of iron or zinc, and are flotilla-shaped ; hence the name of the company. The journey lasts four days and gives one the best impressions of the country. The navigation of the river is very dangerous in consequence of the banks being of white sand, portions of which are continually falling into the water and creating mud banks. However, there is a channel marked with posts, to which anchors are attached. The greatest skill is required in piloting through the narrow defiles. Men are sounding the lead with a rhythmical chant, " Ah mah mah mahlay," in Hindostanee, which rings in one's ears all day. The scenery along the banks is very varied in character. For hours one passes through regions of teak forests, stretching as far as the eye can reach, in undulating fashion like ocean billows. Then ranges of jungle-covered hills appear to approach the river and recede again giving place to wild jungle, large tracts of paddy fields and the petroleum oil region. The river is five miles in breadth in some places, and large petroleum oil barges built of teak, and with carved sterns raised very high in the air upon which the look-out man is seated, are always going up and down stream. The whole country side is covered with the bell-shaped pagodas in clusters of, sometimes, a hundred together and at Pagán, the ancient capital of Upper Burmah, no fewer than 9,999 are supposed to exist; at all events they occupy a stretch of eight miles along the river bank. The chief industry of the people at this place is an inferior kind of lacquered woodwork, made of the bamboo wood canes and ornamented with curious devices and various patterns. Large numbers of Burmese women were seated along the banks as we passed, smoking their large cigars and selling these boxes.

The steamers often run on to the shifting banks of sand in the river and we made no exception. About five o'clock on the second day's trip, our vessel which draws four-and-half feet of water ran aground on to three-and-half feet. Quickly a large anchor weighing four tons was placed on board a boat and dropped about 150 yards from the ship. The ship's windlass made the hawser connection tight and then began the tug of war between the ship and the anchor, in which, as a rule, the ship wins. With engines full speed astern we pulled and pulled, but unavailingly, and the contest was given over for that night. About six o'clock the next morning the fight was resumed. The ship seemed to throb painfully as if to burst, slowly she commenced to vibrate and we slipped gently off into the deep channel and were on our way, while the lead men commenced the weird musical four-note refrain again. The navigation of the river is too dangerous at night, and we therefore always anchored off some picturesque village or small town just before dusk, thus giving us an opportunity of having a walk on shore.

Prome possesses the second largest pagoda in Burmah, a mass of bright gold, standing on a hill and surrounded by hundreds of lesser shrines, in which, sitting and recumbent Buddhas, with serious, laughing or humorous expressions on their faces, are to be seen. One ascends an avenue of carved woodwork under which models of Gautama, all kinds of dolls, candles, and flowers are sold as offerings of propitiation at any given shrine, at the top of which is a large open stone platform, and in the centre stands the pagoda, shaped like a bell, being surmounted by the laced work tee or umbrella. Round it are grouped small temples, in front of which, ascetics, women, men, and children are praying. Why they pray to Buddha is a mystery, as he has entered Nirvána and can neither pray for them nor intercede.*

At Prome we reluctantly quitted the "China," after four days spent on this charming river, and returned by train to Rangoon. This city is celebrated for its winding lakes, round which are gardens and a prettily laid out park, with bungalows of the European residents, and for its glorious Golden Pagoda, situated about one mile from the city on a hill. It is the largest edifice of its kind in the world and is built in the form of a colossal golden bell, 300 feet high, at the top of which a "Tee" is placed of solid gold, ornamented with precious stones. The entrance is guarded by two huge griffins of brick, painted white. Passing these, one

---

* Those who are interested in the Buddhist religion will find a short epitome of the life of Gautama, and the principal doctrines, at the end of this work (taken from a pamphlet issued by a Madras Society).

enters a gateway, painted in vermilion and gold, covered with hideous representations of the Buddhistic tortures reserved for the damned; and after mounting a dilapidated stone staircase covered with carved Burmese wood arcades, under which lepers and beggars with distorted features are usually grouped, one reaches the immense stone terrace, a thousand feet square in the centre of which stands the pagoda. It is built of solid masonry tapering to a spire, covered with gold. The gold is said to equal the weight of a Burmese king. The whole building is a blaze of gold and is most dazzling to the eyesight. Surrounding it are many temples containing images of Gautama, in all shapes and sizes and with varieties of expressions, built of marble, alabaster, solid brass, and gilded wood; some holding paper or silk umbrellas. All kinds of flowers, some of them preserved in bottles, and white paper flags are offered, while candles burn before favourite shrines. Round the enclosure hang large numbers of handsome carved brass gongs, the largest of which is called " The Great Bell of Rangoon," and weighs 40 or 50 tons. It hangs in one corner, and a large trunk of a tree, suspended from ropes in a horizontal position, is used by pilgrims to sound this bell. It is a part of their religion to call the attention of the gods in this manner.

This pagoda derives its especial sanctity from being the depository of the relics of the last four Buddhas. A pagoda is not in itself a temple, but a monument erected to the everlasting memory of Gautama, and that is why so many thousands are seen over the country, giving the impression somewhat of its being a gigantic cemetery.

Rangoon itself is now the third largest

port in the East and is daily increasing in importance. The trade in rice is enormous, and John Chinaman having settled down in the city commands the principal trade. The traffic in timber is one of the principal industries, and elephants are used in the timber yards for bringing the timber from the riverside and stacking it in regular heaps. The elephant is most sagacious, and it is an extraordinary sight to see the easy manner in which he turns over large trunks of trees, pushes them into line with his head and then telescopes them, one after the other.

On Sunday morning, the 26th February, we left Rangoon by a steam launch aptly named the "Pagoda," which took us down stream, where we boarded the steamship "Pentakota," bound for Penang and Singapore, but calling at Moulmein to take in a cargo of rice. At ten o'clock the anchor weighed and we were dropping down the Rangoon river with the ebb tide, watching the sun's rays gilding the spire of the Golden Pagoda, which soon disappeared from view. By one o'clock we were out in the open sea, and when dusk set in our skipper decided to drop anchor near the entrance of the Moulmein river, as the channel is too dangerous for navigation at night. As I write, the rattle of the chains announces to us that this is done, and we sleep to-night really "rocked in the cradle of the deep."

At 6.30 this, Monday, morning, we entered the river, passing beautifully-wooded islets, covered with green mango trees, ferns and palms, and in a few hours were anchored again about six miles from Moulmein, which we can see up the river nestling round a wooded hill, while around us are numerous rice mills, from which we proceed to embark our large cargo of 23,000 bales of rice.

March 1st.—Alongside the river are large timber yards employing fifty elephants for moving the timber. This morning we noticed some of them taking their matutinal baths. There are about 500 European residents here and the town possesses a pretty club-house, called a Gymkhana, to which ladies are admitted. Round and about the pagoda are some of the most exquisitely-carved wood houses, beautifully gilded over a back ground of vermilion, and rising in tiers to a tapering point. They are usually the residence of Buddhist phoongyees or monks.

Ivory carving is carried on here, but owing to the great value of elephants' tusks it has languished and good specimens are very difficult to obtain. We saw a beautiful Buddhist bible with carved characters, the ivory being cut in long strips and the covers consisting of the most ornate work representing Buddha, demons, etc., etc.

The Burmese are an interesting race but are very indolent, and allow the Chinese to usurp all the best trade in the bazaars, and Tamils and other low caste Hindoos to do the drudgery. They are however proverbial for hospitality, and where a Hindoo would allow you to perish of hunger in the jungle rather than give you shelter in his hut,—which he will not do, because of his obnoxious caste scruples,—a Burmese would give you the best corner to sleep in and allow you to remain as his guest as long as you please. In fact this Eastern hospitality has in many cases been grossly abused by impecunious Europeans. Quaint stories are told of their simple nature. When the first railway was built, the natives entered the station, and as is usual when entering a house, they took off their boots when going into the railway cars, which they mistook for rooms; off went the train, leaving the boots in rows on the platform.'

Just opposite the town, in the Salwen river, is a large and beautifully wooded island, the British ownership of which soon after the annexation of Moulmein in 1852, was disputed by the Burmese. In order therefore to settle the matter finally the following plan was hit upon:—

At a given point a few miles up the river, a cocoanut was thrown into the stream. If the nut was carried by the current outside the island, the land would become ours and if inside in front of Moulmein, it would remain native possession. Needless to say the astute British officer knew perfectly well which way the current flowed, and so in this easy manner, the island was added to the British Crown.

In Moulmein we were hospitably entertained by Mr. Orr, in his charming bungalow, during over two days' stay, and were taken for some pleasant drives into the country.

March 3rd.—Anchor is weighed and we bid adieu to Burmah. The " Pentakota " drops swiftly with the tide down the river, and slowly a projecting wooded hill shuts out lovely Moulmein from our view. We pass along for a couple of hours between banks of rich virgin tropical vegetation and are soon on our voyage to Penang. During the afternoon we threaded our way through the Malgui archipelago of islands, in which large numbers of the edible birds' nests are found, which the Chinese find so delectable.

March 5th.—We are just entering Penang

harbour. On the left, a long low line of dense cocoanut palms, behind which rises a range of pale blue coloured mountains culminating in the Kedar Peak, which ascends abruptly from the sea to an altitude of 5,000 feet. This is the extreme end of the Asiatic peninsula. On the right, on a flat piece of land lies Penang, embowered in beautiful tamarind trees behind which are lovely hills covered with jungle. From these hills a glorious view of the whole of the Prince of Wales' island, with peeps of the ocean, and of the Straits of Malacca are seen. On landing, japanned jinrickshas, with curious devices in gold, and drawn by Chinese coolies conveyed us to the Oriental hotel. The vegetation is intensely tropical, the most beautiful tree being the flowering flamboyant with gorgeous scarlet blooms. Chinamen usurp the whole of the trade and they deserve it, because of their great business capacity, and shrewdness. The Malays, like the aborigines of Ceylon, the Singhalese, and the Burmese, are too indolent to work, and allow strangers to cater for the modern trade. Even the coolie work is done by the Klings, another name for the Tamils, who come from Southern India. Handsome houses inhabited by wealthy Chinese stand in lovely gardens. These houses have quaint porticos, with gilded doors, flanked right and left with inscriptions in vermillion and gold in Chinese characters, and ornamented with large sized lanterns, in white and red. Opium traffic is largely carried on. We visited an opium farm, and were shown the balls covered with dry poppy leaves in their natural state, as they are received from India, and before being boiled in the large kitchens. In its liquid state as sold to the dealers, it presents the appearance of thick black treacle and is very expensive; a small bottle of it, containing an ounce, costing two dollars. We then entered a so called opium den, where numbers of Chinese were reclining on raised floors and smoking. They seemed to be in a happy lethargic state and were thoroughly enjoying themselves.

Close by, in an open square, a Chinese theatrical performance was being given gratis to the people. The performance was very comical. Only men act, who impersonate women, and the acting goes on for hours. A large table was placed on the stage and covered with a cloth, as a representation of a house. An elderly Chinese lady accompanied by an attendant, then appeared, and after a few minutes of absurd posturing and singing in a falsetto voice, pitched at a key impossible for Europeans, went indoors, by disappearing under the table.

Then an alarm of fire was raised and several men carrying lighted gridirons ran round the table. The old lady was dragged forth and taken away, and for some inexplicable reason, a dirty beggar was substituted in her place. Then a mandarin arrived, who stamped and swore and fumed round the stage, while the onlookers produced from under the table the charred remains of the old beggar, which the distracted mandarin imagined to be those of his mother. Whether he had plotted the destruction of his mamma in this way and was foiled, or not, we cannot say. We came away deeply impressed, but fortunately the melancholy catastrophe did not impair our appetite for tiffin, the chef d'œuvre of which was a superb Malay curry.

March 7th. In the evening about 5.30 we steamed out of the harbour, witnessing a beautiful sunset, but in a few minutes, we ran into a tropical rain-storm, accompanied with thunder and lightning, which effectually shut out from us the retrospective view of Penang.

March 8th. At sea, running through the crowded waters of the Straits of Malacca, a comical incident happened just after leaving Penang. A milk cow we had taken on board, charged into the saloon, butted at the frightened stewards, who jumped upon the tables, ran right round the room and out at the other door. Before we had got over our surprise she appeared again, and ruined a chair this time. Eventually the animal was lassoed, taken forward, and we breathed again. This morning we had fresh milk for breakfast.

March 9th. At seven o'clock we entered the narrow, wooded, serpentine channel, barely 500 feet broad, leading to the harbour of Singapore, with pretty islands dotted here and there, and were soon alongside the jetty. Singapore has now a population of about 200,000, composed of British, Malays, Chinese, Japanese, Eurasians, etc., but is not very interesting apart from its rank and tropical vegetation. The botanical gardens exhibit the most splendid and varied collection of palms and foliage trees, and possess beautiful open air orchid and fern houses, in which these flowers and ferns are seen to perfection. The Governor's house, or rather palace, stands on a high hill, in a fine park, and is a handsome edifice. Lunching at the Singapore club and dining at the Hotel de l' Europe, filled up our day on shore, and early next morning we were on board the

North German mail steamer, "Sachsen," of 4,650 tons, and bound for Hong Kong and Shanghai. Round the vessel are boats, full of white and pink corals, all kinds of shells from the South Sea islands, from the pearly nautilus to the homely cowrie, which are offered at tempting prices. Bartering over, at 9.30 we leave the jetty, while the German band on board plays an inspiriting air. In a few minutes we are abreast of our old friend the "Pentakota," to whose officers we wave adieu; and Singapore, its merchant ships, and its surrounding islands fringed with the eternal palms, slowly disappear as we sail out into the ocean.

CHAPTER VI.

China Sea—Hong Kong—Canton—Its Life—Macao—
Fantan at Macao—Home of Luiz de Camoens—
Return to Hong Kong—Pidgin English—Chinese
Theatre — Poetry — Departure for Shanghai —
Shanghai—China Town in Shanghai.

ARCH 11*th*.—The China seas are visited by tropical rainstorms which burst suddenly, last a few minutes, and immediately afterwards one sails in brilliant sunshine. It is our fate to be just too early to be out of the track of the north-east monsoon, so this morning the "Sachsen" is pitching heavily, a high sea is running, and very few passengers are observable, in fact, everything and everybody are subdued on board.

March 12*th.*—The monsoon still continues, but the sea has subsided somewhat.

March 13*th.*—We just experience a slight rocking motion, like a gentle lullaby after a storm. Our vessel has taken a more southerly course than is usual, outside a dangerous line of reefs called the Paracels, the usual track being inside it. By taking this circuitous route, the total distance from Singapore is increased to over 1,400 miles, and after a calm day, we arrive at 7 a.m. on March 14th, at the north entrance to the harbour of Hong Kong. The passage is narrow, and on both sides overhang high ranges of precipitous mountains; that on the right being the mainland of China, and on the east the island of Hong Kong.

Rounding the point, the harbour lies before us, full of liners, merchantmen, Chinese junks and sampans, with brown ribbed sails, and upon which whole families of Chinese live; while white painted steam launches dart to and fro, making altogether a hubbub of interesting native life. High above us rise the heights, under which the town nestles, conspicuous among them being the peak, to which the inhabitants resort during the hot months, and up which a small tramway can be seen crawling. Soon we are ashore with our goods and chattels, and enter the new palatial Hong Kong hotel built on the jetty, and containing no fewer than 300 bedrooms. Hong Kong island has been called "the land of fragrant streams." The streams we have not yet seen, but certainly we have inhaled the fragrance of the Chinese themselves, which is easily observable to those even whose olfactory nerves are not easily offended. The town crowds round the port, and stretches up the steep hills in an uncomfortable sort of way. In the streets and above the harbour the usual mode of conveyance is by jinricksha, while sedan chairs, carried on long bamboo poles, borne by Chinese coolies, are used to carry passengers up the steep roads and lanes to the higher levels, where the bungalows are situated. Our first experience in a sedan was strange. We mounted, and desired to be taken to the Board of Works, but after half an hour's ride we arrived at the tramway station of the peak, and were unceremoniously set down. After expostulation, on we jogged, and turned up at the Government house. As this did not suit us, on we trotted, and were eventually landed triumphantly at Police Station, No. 9.

Chinese bazaars and native streets are bright with gorgeous lanterns and quaint signs in gold and vermilion, hanging lengthwise, like pieces of Indian ink, and the shops are clean and well kept. At night, when the lanterns are illuminated, the streets present the appearance of being in a perpetual state of carnival. The women all wear ornaments of jade,—a pale green-stone, resembling opal,—both as earrings and bracelets. Good jade is very expensive, and is always worn, as it is considered to bring good luck. The appearance of both sexes is exceedingly neat and orderly, and nothing tawdry is worn. In fact the whole population here is seen in a constant state of work of some kind or other, and is far cleaner in general appearance than the lower classes of Italians in their populous cities.

Embarking in the steamer "Fanshaw," at

five o'clock in the evening of March 18th, we sailed up the Canton river during the night, and arrived off the city at 5.30 in the morning. There were over 2,000 Chinese on board, who are conveyed at a uniform charge of twenty cents each. The river swarmed with a mass of sampans and junks crowded with Chinese families, who live on board and are sheltered by a kind of arch of bamboo matting, stretched over bent laths. Women row and steer these boats with children tied to their backs. At six o'clock I was awakened by a boat woman appearing at my window, and saying, in pidgin English, "Hong Kong you go back to nightee?" To which I replied, "No." "You go see Canton?" "Yes." "This evening I show you nice flower boatee." "You want know my name? Susan."* So we made

---
* Pronounced "Shusan"

the appointment with Susan, who in the meantime took charge of our luggage, while we proceeded on shore with our guide Fong. Fong is a wily celestial who has travelled, and speaks English with a decided matter-of-fact Yankee twang. He headed our procession of sedan chairs upon which we were carried through the city. Canton has a population of perhaps 2,000,000 people, but as Chinese architecture is still in a very primitive condition, and has made no progress for 1000 years, their houses consisting solely of lath and plaster one and two storied erections, the interest of the city for the stranger lies in the street life, bazaars and temples. We soon found ourselves in a labyrinth of narrow lanes and alleys from six to eighteen feet wide, presenting, however, a mass of wonderful colouring, with the various coloured hanging boards suspended from the shops, and filling up the perspective as far as the eye can reach. These alleys stretch for miles in all directions, and the shops in them represent all the well known handicraft trades of China; viz., hand silk weaving, ivory carving, fan making, filigree black wood work, porcelain factories, embroideries, shoe-makers, etc. Thousands of men jostle our chairs, the coolies constantly calling for the road to be cleared. The temple of 500 Genii was the first sight. These are gilded wood figures of Chinese, sitting in rows, and their faces represent all kinds of expressions. In the centre sits the Emperor, and in front of each god are small vases, in which the joss sticks are burned as offerings. Outside this temple were four immense gods who are supposed to guard it. We next went to the temple of horrors, where groups of painted wooden figures vividly depicted punishments of all kinds. Sawing a man in two between two boards; boiling oil; large heated bell descending upon a man; being transferred into an animal, etc., etc. Round these temples crowds of fortune tellers plied their trade, while the joss stick sellers did a lucrative business. The Chinese are clever pisciculturists and large numbers of dried fish shops were observed; live fish, weighing from five to ten pounds, also abounded in tubs outside the shops. Some of the shops have finely carved woodwork, always plants in pots, either camellias, or azaleas, and perhaps a singing bullfinch, or a Tientsin lark. They have also windows, as Chinese thieves have otherwise a happy knack of hooking things on to the end of a long pole, and promptly disappearing. The prison was a wretched structure, with separate compartments for men and women.

There were men with large wooden stocks round their heads, and they wore their hair "un-pigtailed," and looked extremely wild. As they vociferously asseverated that they were insufficiently fed, we threw them some of the loose China cash, for which they exhibited distinct signs of pleasure and thankfulness. As we approached the women's section, a clamouring more resembling that of a flock of geese was heard, but on entering, silence reigned immediately. Among them was one tall, good-looking woman just sentenced to the Ling chi for capital punishment, for poisoning her husband. She had feet about two inches long, One hears a good deal of the hundreds of distinct smells of Cologne, which is a great libel by Coleridge upon that city. Coleridge ought to have written an ode upon Canton. The smells from the decaying refuse in the stagnant water pools would have frightened the witch of Endor herself. A seven-storied pagoda we next visited, and a water clock 600 years old. Four large copper tanks were arranged like steps, and from each, water dropped, marking the seconds, while through a slit in the lowest receptacle, a measure marked with the hours rose each minute. Then we ascended a portion of the old city wall to the five-storied pagoda, at the top of which, in the company of several josses or gods seated beside us, we partook of tiffin. Several Chinese ladies prayed very devoutly to two twin brothers with long black beards. We also had an audience of thirty inquisitive gaping Chinese, who, when we had finished, speedily devoured the remains of our repast. Having luncheon in a temple in the company of heathen gods, while the natives were drinking tea and smoking, was a novelty. On the south side in descending, a Chinese cemetery was to be seen, stretched over several hills, with the tombs all built in the shape of horse-shoes. Passing through Jade street, where the exhibits of jade stone worn by the women are sold, we crossed over a bridge into the Shameen quarter of the city, to the English concession. The Roman Catholics have built a large cathedral in Canton and have very many proselytes, but the great obstacle to the spread of Christianity is ancestor worship, which in reality is—filial piety gone mad.

Chinese believe that the spirits stand in the same need of comfort and necessaries as the inhabitants of this world, and therefore offer them all kinds of imitation houses, boats, food, etc., all of which are burned. They also send supplies to beggar-spirits, as propitiation for neglect by living relatives. There are three powerful religions, viz., Confucianism,

Buddhism and Taouism, and a pious Chinaman can belong to all three In fact their religion is a strong combination of superstition and philosophies. In the Shameen quarter a decent European hotel is built, where we dined and afterwards went off in Susan's sampan to see the flower-boats These are houses built on floating barges, moored in the river, furnished with gorgeous Chinese embroideries, inlaid mother of pearl carved furniture, magnificent gasaliers and lanterns, and are frequented by opulent Chinese. Girls with their faces painted white and rose colour, with lips like cherry blossom, and wearing the jade stone ornaments, play on the pei-pei or native guitar, accompanied with falsetto singing, for the edification of their audience. Gaping crowds of lower class Chinese stand on the footways between the barges, and gaze at all these splendours. At dusk, which is about eight o'clock according to Chinese ideas, trumpets are blown and two small guns are fired, at the gates of the city, and at nine o'clock the gates are closed entirely. The next morning we were awakened at cockcrow by discharges of crackers and squibs in all directions, which continued for more than an hour, and at eight o'clock we proceeded by the steam ship, "White Foam," to the Portuguese settlement of Macao.

The country for the first few miles was tame and uninteresting, only rice fields with an occasional pagoda, similar in shape to those in Kew Gardens, being visible, until we reached the mouth of the Tigris, where a large and fortified fort called Boccatigris, meaning mouth of the Tigris, built by German engineers, was situated. Rounding this in a short time Macao came into sight, lying in a land-locked bay, with a half circle of houses stretching round it, and reminding one of a Riviera watering place ; with its picturesque lighthouse perched upon a hill to the right, and its bold promontory of brown rocks on the left side. Sailing round this headland we entered the harbour, where large numbers of piratical looking craft and junks carrying small cannon were at anchor. Landing here we drove through clean streets all bearing Portuguese names ; in fact the whole place had a continental aspect, the band of the Portuguese regiment playing in the prettily laid-out gardens, while priests with their shovel black hats, perambulated in twos and threes here and there.

In the Chinese quarter are situated the celebrated gambling houses, where the game of fantin is played. There are sixteen of these houses, each paying 10,000 dollars concession to the Portuguese government. The game is very fair. At a large table sit two croupiers, one of whom throws on to the table a quantity of loose cash over which he places a brass cover. Then the players stake on any of four numbers, 1, 2, 3 or 4, and when the stake is completed, the cash is counted out in sections of four, and the number of coins remaining, whether 1, 2, 3 or 4, win, minus 8 per cent. which the bank deducts. As only one number can win, of course the bank receives all the money staked on the other three numbers. Chinese sit smoking in an upper gallery, from which they lower their stakes in a basket.

A celebrated Portuguese poet lived in Macao more than 300 years ago, and we visited the old house and beautiful gardens in which he used to walk and gain inspiration. Large banyan trees threw their knotted roots and gnarled trunks round loose rocks, and in one corner stood the poet's grave; a simple bronze bust, standing on a stone pedestal with the inscription, "Luiz de Camoens, morrea 1530." Over the tomb stood a plain arch made by placing one large rock of granite rudely across two upright pieces, the whole shadowed by trees and festooned with ivy creepers, forming a most natural and poetic mausoleum. Leaving this garden we were conveyed in jinrickshas for six miles to a Chinese walled town named Chin San. It was on Sunday, March 20th, the festival of the moon, and the people were letting off crackers in all directions, accompanied by vigorous gong sounding, to exorcise evil spirits, and were also offering roast pig and other delicacies at the gaudily decorated joss houses or temples, (made simply of bamboo matting), in the streets. We were carried along a narrow uneven road, lined with prickly pear, cactus and bamboo trees, through a Portuguese arch, erected in August, 1849, dividing the Portuguese territory from China proper. Shortly afterwards we passed the custom house, in front of which floated a large yellow flag, with a dragon on it, the emblem of the Emperor. Crowds of people pressed to and fro, very quaintly dressed and carrying pale blue umbrellas. On entering the walls we at last arrived at a palace, built and kept up by the relatives of a deceased mandarin, named Low Sai Kut, where his spirit might wander about at its own sweet will, when he desired to revisit this earthly sphere. His opium couch was all ready for his reception, and servants were in charge to minister to his wants. The rooms were furnished with carved ebony wood furniture, handsome porcelain vases and bronzes, and upon the walls hung valuable tapestries and embroideries. In the garden was a tea-house, where tea was served to us in the Chinese fashion, viz., an infusion of undried tea leaves and stalks and hot water, without either milk or sugar.

The origin of tea drinking in China is interesting; water is man's natural beverage, but in this country it is so bad that the Chinese mind perceived the necessity of boiling it to kill the germs. This again being insipid, the leaves of the tea plant were discovered and found to give the water a pleasant flavour, hence the general custom of tea drinking. The gardens are kept in scrupulous order, and beautiful yellow tea roses were offered to us. Having thus partaken of the hospitality of the departed mandarin we were carried back to Macao. The next morning we embarked on board the steamship "Shahsan," for Hong Kong again, At eight punctually the bells ring, a horn is sounded, and we move slowly along the lines of junks, sampans and river craft, lying off the jetty, through the brown muddy waters out into the deep blue of the open sea, passing the nine grass-covered, rocky islands, which are the pride of Macao. After a three hours' sail we enter the harbour through the Sulphur Straits, between the Green Islands and Hong Kong Island itself, and are soon on shore. Immediately upon landing, we witnessed a Chinese wedding procession over half-a-mile in length :— dragons, banners, painted temples, and houses, gongs and gong beaters, children painted ghastly colors, etc., and hundreds of men elaborately costumed, composed it.

March 21st.—The streets in Hong Kong are filled with flower sellers, offering the most beautiful roses and violets for a few cents. In fact, the Chinese are exceedingly fond of both flowers and birds, and in most shops camellias or azaleas in full bloom are seen, with an occasional piping bullfinch.

The view from the peak is one of the finest in the world.

The Steam Funicular railway ascends in ten minutes to a gap close to the summit, and is extremely steep, in some parts rising one in two. Looking down from the flagstaff at a height of 1,800 feet above sea level, the harbour presents the appearance of a large picture framed in the steep mountains. Upon a surface of deep blue colour ride the vessels at anchor, surrounded by hundreds of fishing junks. Everything seen from this altitude seems still and lifeless, but suddenly the picture is marred. From a P. & O. liner a long line of black smoke is emitted, which spreads itself across the canvas. The screw revolves and the placidity of the scene is disturbed by the churned up wash of water, as the vessel glides along and away into the offing, homeward bound. Looking southwards, between the grey coloured mountainous islands, stretches the vast expanse of the ocean. Descending we pass the Mount Austin hotel, erected for the convenience of the inhabitants during the hot season.

"Pidgin English," the language spoken by the Chinese, has now a small literature of its own, and is composed of a mixture of English, Portuguese, and Chinese words. "Chop, chop," means "quickly," "chin, chin," "good day," "chow, chow," "food." Here is a selected sentence, "Hong Kong side hab got too muchee piecee Chinaman," means there are too many Chinese in Hong Kong. A Chinaman when asked why the bow of his sampan was adorned with two large eyes, replied, "Sampan, if have no eye, how fashion can see, can walkee." Some local residents have amused a leisure hour by putting some gems of English literature into this jargon. The soliloquy in Hamlet, for example, commencing in this way. "Can do, no can do, how fashion." Here is Longfellow's celebrated Excelsior in Pidgin English :—

1.

That rightey tim tim begin chop chop,
One young man walkee, no can stop,
Maskee snow! maskee ice!
He cally flag with chop so nice
    Topside Galow.

2.

He too muchee solly, one piecee eye
Look see sharp, so, all same my
He talkey largey, talkey stlong
Too muchee culio all same gong
    Topside Galow.

3.

Inside that house he look see light
And evely toom got five all light
He look see plenty ice more high
Inside he mouth he plenty cly
    Topside Galow.

4.

Olo man talkee, no can walk
By mby lain come, welly dark,
Hab got water, welly wide;
Maskee! my wantchey go topside
    Topside Galow.

5.

"Man, man" one girley talkee he;
What for you go topside look see?
And one time more he plenty cly
But allo tim walkee plenty high
    Topside Galow.

6.

Take care that spoilee thee, young man,
Take care that ice, he want man, man;
That coolie chin chin he " Good Night "
He talkee, my can go at light.
        Topside Galow.

7.

Joss Pidgin man he soon begin,
Morning time that Joss chin chin,
He no man see, he plenty fear,
Cos some man talkee, he can hear
        Topside Galow.

8.

That young man die, one large dog see
To muchee bobbely findee he,
His hand blong colo, all same ice
Hab got he flag, with chop so nice,
        Topside Galow.

The Chinese people are, without doubt, the Imperial race of the Orient. Their ultra-conservatism is their great drawback, and it is lamentable that such a fine country should not be opened up by railways. The difficulty of locomotion in the interior is enormous, If a road has to be carried over a mountain, instead of its being made in zigzags, it is carried clean up a height of 1,500 feet and down again, and at its best it is but a simple track, over which only bullock carts can pass. To a new arrival from the West, there appears to be a remarkable sameness in all the people. They all have black hair, black eyes, with clean shaven heads and faces, and present so much uniformity that the question arises: How can one possibly distinguish one from the other? But a few months' residence in the country shows there are many points of difference, and, if a proof of this assertion were needed, one has only to instance that the Chinese hold the same opinion about ourselves. They have many peculiarities. Out of door games are seldom indulged in. The most violent form of amusement in which adults engage, is shuttlecock played with the feet. A more sedentary pastime is kite flying in which grown-up men indulge while children look on. A visit to a Chinese theatre is a study in character itself. Theatrical exhibitions are often connected with religion, for they are often held in honor of a god's birthday. The performances last sometimes for three days, with intervals for eating and sleeping. The stage is bareness itself. A few chairs and tables can be made to represent palaces, houses, or almost anything. A frail structure composed of piled up chairs and tables can easily be made to represent lofty crags and precipitous mountains, over which the heroine can easily clamber. No curtain falls between the acts, and assistants are continually walking about on the stage bringing in or taking out accessories required during the performances. The villain always has a white nose, and men always impersonate women. The dresses are often most gorgeous; robes of gilt brocade, with long feathers, several feet in length, falling from the hats of the performers, while flags are worn projecting from their backs, and these costumes atone somewhat for the want of *mise en scene*. All the actors walk in at one door, advance to a mat thrown down in front, perhaps of a table and two chairs, go through their roles with violent gesticulation, and falsetto singing in a kind of recitative, march off again out at the left door. The hero can always be told from his martial air or blustering swagger. At the end of certain speeches or passages, loud clashings of the cymbals and discordant beatings of gongs announce the fact to the audience. Whatever may happen on the stage, the Chinese stolid man or woman never betrays any form of emotion, and their countenances never alter. They take everything "*au grand serieux.*"

The people consume the flesh of cats and dogs largely, but pork is the chief meat in the south, while fish and fowl are largely eaten. That of the chow chow dog is considered a great delicacy, while that of the cat resembles rabbit. A cheap meal can be obtained for one cent. by an impecunious Celestial, consisting of two plates of succulent rats meat, boiled rice and two cups of tea. Fans are used largely by both sexes, and young Chinese gentlemen carry them in place of a walking stick, as it gives them something to hold and to gesticulate with. Schoolmasters use them to rap a boy over the head. Nearly 2,000 years ago, a lady of the court, when deserted by her royal master, sent him a fan with the following lines upon it, which have been rendered into English by Dr. Martin, as follows :—

LINES INSCRIBED ON A FAN.

Written by Pan Tsieh Yu, a lady of the Court and presented to the Emperor Ching Ti, of the Han Dynasty, before Christ 18.

> Of fresh new silk, all snowy white,
> And round as harvest moon,
> A pledge of purity and love,
> A small but welcome boon.

While summer lasts, borne in the hand,
　Or folded on the breast,
'Twill gently soothe thy burning brow,
　And charm thee to thy rest.

But ah! when Autumn frosts descends,
　And Autumn winds blow cold,
No longer sought, no longer loved,
　'Twill lie in dust and mould.

This silken fan then deign accept,
　Sad emblem of my lot!
Caressed and cherished for an hour,
　Then speedily forgot!

In consequence of this, a deserted wife is often jocularly called "an autumn fan," by the Chinese.

The Cantonese boatmen, in rainy weather, present the appearance of veritable "Robinson Crusoes." They attire themselves in capes and trousers made of dried bamboo leaves, and wear enormous straw hats a yard in diameter.

The music, is to European ears, most barbarous and without harmony, but the Chinese do not appreciate *our* music, any more than we do theirs. A Chinaman listening to the military band in Hong Kong was asked his opinion of it, and he said that it lacked harmony. That they fully appreciate their own music needs but a glance at the crowd round a Chinese band to discover. Their writings also show this, as seen from the following extract from " Gems of Chinese Literature : "—

"Softly as the whisper of murmured words; now loud and soft together, like the patter of pearls and pearlets dropping upon a marble dish. Or, liquid, like the warbling of the Mango bird in the bush, trickling like the streamlet on its downward course. And like the torrent, stilled by the grip of frost, so for a moment was the music lulled in a passion too deep for words."

After that, no one can say the Chinese have no ear for music.

The Chinese have several names; they keep their surnames through life, but at every memorable event, such as going to school, or getting married, they take another one.

The East is the land of poetry. Unfortunately Chinese poetry is almost incapable of adequate translation. The most celebrated poet was Li-Taipo, whose works were published in thirty volumes. He lived in the 10th century, during the Tanj dynasty, which is described as the Augustan age in poetry and letters. He is described by one writer as—

"The best known of China's countless host of lyric poets, famous for his excellent imagery, his wealth of words, his telling allusions to the past, and for the musical cadence of his verse."

Here is a specimen put into English :—

"A VISIT TO THE RAPIDS OF THE WHITE RIVER."

"I cross the stream just as it starts to life,

From man and all his deeds afar I roam.

The isles are clad in nature's living hues,

And set in scenes of sweetest beauty rare.

The deep blue sky is mirrored in the stream,

Whose broad expanse reflects the passing clouds.

I watch them as they sail away to sea.

My leisured mind next wanders where the stream

Is full of fish that dart adown its course,

The setting sun doth end my day long songs,

By silvery moonlit rays I hie me home

To where my humble cot a-field doth lie."

We start to-day for Shanghai and the Inland sea of Japan, in the Canadian Pacific Company's liner, the "Empress of Japan," which is now lying in the harbour. She is one of three sister ships, called the three "Empresses" which were built at Barrow-in-Furness, specially for passenger service between Canada, Japan and China, thus connecting the West with the far East. Speed and strength were the first considerations, and with their steel hulls, double bottoms, watertight compartments, twin screws, triple expansion engines and a record of nineteen knots an hour, they are very successful for the service. They are painted white, making between decks a difference of many degrees in temperature. They are 485 feet in length, 50 feet beam, and carry 150 first class passengers. All cabins, state rooms and decks are illuminated with the electric light generated from four dynamos. Chinese servants in caps and snowy blouses minister automatically to one's wants. Everybody goes on board in a small launch, towing behind it a Chinese junk conveying luggage. At twelve o'clock on Wednesday, March 22nd, we slowly steam away. There are 800 or more Chinese on board, bound for Vancouver, whence they will endeavour to smuggle themselves across the Canadian frontier into the United States. Their departure is signalized by a discharge of crackers in a basket suspended from the top of the mast of a small sampan. The mists and fogs announcing the approach of the Hong Kong summer are lying low down under the sides of the yellowish brown mountains, against whose rocks the surf is grandly beating. Our speed is soon accelerated as we leave the channel of the Lye-moon pass, and enter the open sea. It is rough, but the vessel forces her way through the waves, as if flying through space and very little motion is perceptible.

March 23rd.—In the Straits of Formosa. These are crowded waters. Chinese trawling junks are dancing over the waves, always in pairs. We almost fly past the "Tyiune," a liner of 2,000 tonnage, from Australia which left Hong Kong two days previously, bound for Shanghai, and which is pitching and rolling in the heavy sea.

March 24th.—About six o'clock in the evening we arrived at the Woosung bar, at the mouths of the rivers Yang-tsze and Hoang-ho which here unite, forming a fine harbour. The coast is simply a low brown line, behind which the river can be seen curving round to Shanghai, fourteen miles distant. This bar is called the Heavenly Barrier, and during the French war of 1884, the Chinese made it more effectual than ever by sinking stone laden junks across all but one narrow channel. Thirteen years ago there was a railway from Woosung to Shanghai, but the Chinese bought it at a great price, tore up the rails, and threw them with the locomotives into the river. On the morning of the 26th at seven o'clock a steam tender took most of the passengers off to spend a day in Shanghai. As we steam up the river, we notice along the banks, high walled villages crowned with the fantastical roofs of an occasional joss house or temple, and soon we are abreast of the Chinese fleet of six men of war, a French spick-and-span turret ship, an American armed cruiser and a couple of German gunboats; protecting the interests of their several nations. Proas and junks with ribbed and laced brown sails go by, with large staring eyes painted at all the bows, for "If have no eye, no can savez, how can see go," says the wise Chinaman. Dirty, fierce visaged, pig-tailed crews peer from the decks between the matting and bamboo poles. The river here describes another bend and we come in sight of the city, which has a most imposing appearance. The river is full of shipping and the principal street is called the Bund, being built in the form of an embankment upon the river, with fine promenades and avenues of trees. Handsome six storied buildings are built along this.

There are really three Shanghais, the English settlement and the French forming separate towns, and divided from each other and from the Chinese Town by canals of water. The French compound might be a bit of Paris itself. The French have all French nomenclature and French policemen, while the English streets are named Nanking road, Pekin road, Bubbling Well road, etc., and are guarded by picked stalwart Sikhs, from Afghanistan, wearing red turbans. One must never ask an European resident in the town of Shanghai to escort you to the native city, for a refusal will assuredly be met with. He may have been there once, but it is better not to speak to him on the subject at all. But the enterprising tourist is there to see life, manners and customs; so nothing daunted, we lit our manillas and braved the smells, and entered the city walls. The same offensive effluvia, as in Canton, with the stagnant pools and ponds and decaying refuse must be accepted, if you wish to dive into the seven-foot lanes and alleys. Everybody remembers the coloured pictures of the Chinese tea houses, as seen on the wall-papers, fans and vases; of the tea shops, with the little bridges, picturesque grottoes and blue water underneath. We rejoiced therefore, greatly, when our guide told us, that he could show us a mandarin's tea-house. Well, we arrived, and it was all there, winding grottoes, quaint tea-houses, with carved roofs, curious little bridges, all built certainly over water, but water of a stagnant green and alarming putridity, while the houses were dirty and almost deserted. We then went to a curious temple, with large carved wooden gods and junks, before whom more roasted pig was being offered. One of the priests kindly burnt some pieces of silver paper, before a fierce looking god, to wish us "good luck" on our voyage. We were then hurried off to see some Chinese gold fish in large tanks, which were filled with green water, through which we could see large numbers of them. The dragon fish was the most peculiar, with four revolving tails like the screw of a ship, and a large head, with no body; also a small fish, with large goggle eyes, projecting from the head. At last, tired of Chinese life and its smells, we returned to French Shanghai, had tiffin at the Hotel des Colonies, and returned in our steam launch, with an influx of new passengers going to Japan, to the Woosung Bar, where the "Empress" was lying.

This (Sunday) morning we are steaming across the Yellow Sea, in beautiful calm weather, and after muster of the ship's crew on the middle deck, morning service was held. I have before mentioned that there are nearly 1,000 Chinese on board, bound for Vancouver, berthed both fore and aft, and packed three deep, but no one is brave enough to venture down to view the mass of Mongolian humanity, as we are content to watch now and then the hundred or so, that are allowed at intervals to amuse themselves in the fore deck by playing dominoes and taking the air. The ships' doctor, has had the arduous task of vaccinating the whole of the men yesterday and to-day.

CHAPTER VII.

ARRIVAL IN JAPAN—NAGASAKI—THE INLAND SEA—KOBE —OZAKA—NARA—KEGURA DANCE—JINRICKSHA TO KYOTO—KYOTO—YAAMIS' HOTEL—GEISHA DANCE.

E awoke this morning to find ourselves in the land of the Rising Sun, at anchor before lovely Nagasaki. We were lying in a beautiful bay, round which nestled the town surrounded by odd-shaped hills covered with fresh spring green. Hundreds of little Japanese men and women were soon clambering up the sides of our ship, like monkeys, delivering, in small baskets, 1,700 tons of coal. It was rather a primitive way of doing so, but it was really most extraordinary to notice the agility of these bright chattering people, passing the circular baskets holding about 12 lbs. of coal one from another, as they stood on the rungs of the ladders, right into the bunkers. Japan really lies before us at last, and we are soon taken ashore in a gondola-shaped sampan. On landing at the jetty, we are surrounded by a crowd of the Japanese jinricksha men, and are soon bowling along through narrow streets with little houses, and little men and women waddling along with the peculiar noise made by the geta or wooden clogs which they wear, while the women and girls mostly have plump little babies strapped on their backs. As the people are small, so everything is in proportion, and the diminutive must often be employed in describing things Japanese. We soon arrive at a flight of stone steps, which we clamber up, and find ourselves in the open court of a Shinto temple, in the centre of which, is a curious bronze horse; then on up the hill, past large camphor trees and blossoming camellias to a tea house, where saké, a rice spirit, is offered us in tiny cups, also straw coloured tea, drunk without milk or sugar, with little oranges and tiny green and red biscuits, calculated perhaps, to satisfy the appetite of a butterfly, or even of a Japanese; but not an European.

One very small musumé amused us with an absurd posturing dance called the nosuki, and held, while she danced, a mask in front of her face. She was accompanied by the tuneful music of the samisen, a kind of guitar, played by other girls seated on the ground, with a piece of white ivory called a "hashi." From this tea house we ascended to the summit of the hill, and beheld

Nagasaki at our feet, the roofs of the houses looking like card houses.

Nagasaki is celebrated for its tortoise shell carving; and curious models of sampans, jinrickshas, etc. are dexterously carved by boys. After coaling, which was accomplished in a very few hours, the "Empress" left Nagasaki to convey us through the beautiful inland sea of Japan, to our destination, Kobé, and then on to Yokohama, and across the silent Pacific to Vancouver.

At four o'clock we steamed away out of the narrow inlet and winding creeks, past the martyr's rock of great historical interest, from the top of which 1,200 Roman Catholics were hurled into the sea; and then through the narrow straits of Shimoneski into the enclosed bit of ocean called the inland sea, which presents the appearance of a vast lake, surrounded by lofty mountains. The waters were enlivened with fishing craft with small square ribbed sails, and at intervals the coast line narrowed, affording us only just room to pass, then widening again to a width of twenty miles or so.

Unfortunately for us, the day was hazy, and low lying clouds held the views of the mountains from us. At eight o'clock in the evening we sighted the lights of Kobé, and we landed on the morning of March 28th. What a contrast we observed between the stolidity and imperturbability of the Chinamen, and the merriment and jollity depicted in the faces of these Japanese, who persistently set off giggling at nothing at all in particular! Then their courteous ways and polite bows would do credit to Sir Walter Raleigh, or a descendant of the noblesse of France. Even the jinricksha man is not so importunate as the Chinaman, and laughs joyously at receiving his ten cents. for carrying one to the hotel. As we dash up the street, we notice a thick mist still hanging round the hills, and rain commencing to fall. The men were all carrying large umbrellas made of white oil skin, as a protection against it, while the women were shuffling or toddling with a dot and go one sort of step. Our first walk was to a romantic gorge, where were two waterfalls, called the Nibobiki.

March 29*th.*—We started off early by train to visit Ozaka, one hour's distance by rail, and containing half a million inhabitants. The country through which we passed was highly cultivated and irrigated, while rising abruptly to our left was a chain of mountains, with curious volcanic formations. At the railway station a strange clattering noise, resembling castanets, is made on the asphalte paving by the wooden clogs worn by the women.

The city is built on a plain, intersected with numerous rivers and canals, crossed by no fewer than 808 bridges, giving it the appearance somewhat of Venice. The houses are mostly one-storied, and of unpainted wood, and the streets are very long, while telegraph poles and wires are abundant, and the whole place is illumined by the electric light. The great sight is the castle, one of the strongest in the world, with enormous blocks of granite as large as those used in the pyramids, and brought from Nagasaki. Tickets giving permission to view the interior we obtained at the Foreign Office.

There are three moats filled with water, and from the donjon or keep a magnificent view of Ozaka was obtained, while we observed snow lying on the mountains in the distance. Some of the blocks of granite were 20 feet long, and 15 feet high. In the centre formerly stood the most magnificent palace in Japan, but it was burnt during the revolution of 1868. Truly if the Japanese are small in stature, their ideas were great, for this powerful and inaccessible castle is raised stone upon stone from a level plain, and possesses no advantage in natural site, as Heidelberg, Ehrenbreitstein, or Gibraltar.

One of the most beautiful arts of Japan is painting upon porcelain, and we next paid a visit to a celebrated artist, Maizan, and were shown girls and men painting upon Satsuma ware. One small basin had already received 1,008 miniature butterflies, almost all different, and scarcely perceptible to the eye; but seen through a magnifying glass they were most lovely in colouring. The artist knew the exact number he had painted. The very best work is most expensive, and we purchased one tiny piece with coloured chrysanthemums, wistaria and butterflies, for 12½ dollars. This minute painting is most trying for the eyesight.

Returning to Kobé for the night, we started early the next morning on our journey into the interior by taking train to Nara. Strangers arriving in Japan are not allowed to leave the so-called treaty ports without obtaining passports from the Japanese government, and these are only to be obtained for English subjects through the British legation at Tokio. We applied for them at Nagasaki to the English consul, and on landing at Kobé we received them from Tokio. Among the amusing prohibitive regulations enumerated upon them is the following :—

"Travelling at night in a horse carriage without a lantern and attending a fire on horse-back." The price charged for the passport is two dollars.

On entering our railway carriage a Japanese gentleman travelling with two ladies placed at our feet, in a most polite way, a basketful of oranges, and they were intensely amused when we said, "Arigato" (thank you); and in return we offered them cigarettes, in the native vernacular, at which they were delighted. On arriving at Nara we commenced our first experience of a Japanese inn, or yedoya, which merits a description. The house was one storied and built entirely of wood and paper. The rooms are raised about two feet from the ground, and on entering, one's boots must be taken off, in order not to soil the mats. The inn was sufficiently Europeanised to allow of the substitute of slippers being laid over our boots. No furniture whatever was in the rooms as the Japanese eat off the floors, and with chop-sticks, but presently chairs and a round table were brought in and two lighted charcoal bronze braziers called "hibachi," which are the only means of heating these flimsy houses. As glass is expensive, oiled paper is used, and in this small dining room there were four sliding windows with 248 tiny frames of oiled paper. The other three sides of the rooms consisted of eight sliding bamboo matting panels, and four painted panels, and on the floor were four bamboo mats. After dinner some of the sliding panels were withdrawn and in the three next compartments, large mattresses were thrown down on the floor. For covering, two large warm quilts, called futons, are used. One must disabuse one's-self of the idea of obtaining any comfort, as it is known in England, because of the fact that these sliding panels can be opened on both sides, and as Japanese people are very inquisitive, one never knows on which side of the room the next visitor will appear. In my bedroom the furniture consised of a large blue vase with a bunch of cherry blossom, one piece of bronze and a lacquered wood-horse for one's clothes, and the before mentioned bed on the floor. Outside the oil paper panels was a balcony overlooking an artificial lake and gardens, and a fine mountain panorama in the distance. Everything was scrupulously clean and neat in the house. In the morning a panel slid on one side, and the "nezan," or waitress appeared, bringing in morning "cha," or tea, saying, "Ohayo," "good morning," and laughing merrily. It was bitterly cold, and the water for washing being placed on the balcony, we had to wash in turn. As the "nezan" proceeded at the same time to shut up our sliding compartments and to take the "futons," and as no persuasion in the world would make her go away we had to finish dressing as best we could. In a few moments no traces of our bedrooms could be seen.

After breakfast we proceeded to visit the sights of Nara.

The town was the ancient capital from A.D. 709. A large wooden five-storied pagoda, built in 730, is perfectly preserved, and is older than any cathedral in Europe. Just below this was to be seen a large pond full of tame fish and small turtles, and Japanese women sold us some small red puff balls to throw to the fish. The balls float on the water, and the fish in their efforts to seize them, toss them out of the water. This sight is very amusing to the numerous pilgrims who come to visit the sacred shrines and temples hidden away in the glorious woods surrounding the town. The principal temple contains a colossal statue of Dai Butsu, the Japanese equivalent of Buddha, in bronze, 53 feet high. Some idea of the size of this image may be realised, by the fact that in the right hand a statue of Bosatsu is held, 18 feet high. It has a gilded glory behind it, and large lotos flowers and bronzes are placed near. Close to it and adjoining another Buddhist wooden temple with gorgeous interior decorations, hangs one of the three huge bells of Japan. It is $13\frac{1}{2}$ feet high and was cast in A.D. 732. Nearly 36 tons of copper and one ton of tin were used in the casting.

Proceeding further on into the wood, we passed several herds of perfectly tame dun-coloured deer, who accepted biscuits from our hands, and soon arrived at the principal gateway of the famous Shinto temple of Kasuga-no-miya. These gateways are made of timber with lintels thrown across the top and are generally painted vermilion. They are to be seen at the entrances of all Shinto temples all over the country, but the origin of them is now unknown. Before entering this temple a digression must be made to enable me to give a brief account of the Shinto state religion. Shinto means, in the first place, the way of the gods, and inculcates ancestor-worship first, and nature worship afterwards. Its principal theories are, to follow your natural impulses and obey the mikado. As may be imagined the court and state profess Shintoism, and its forms of worship seem closely allied to that of the ancient Druids. The temples are all of unpainted carved wood with thatched roofs, and have no images or external decorations. The ceremonies and forms of worship have been the same for over a thousand years. The Japanese, however, nearly always embrace the two religions of Shintoism and Buddhism, and their temples are built closely together in the same woods as in this instance at Nara. After its birth every child is placed under the care of some Shinto deity, but is generally buried with the elaborate ritual of Buddhist religion. In fact there are very few real Buddhists or Shintoists. When approaching a temple, a worshipper calls the attention of the gods by clapping his hands, sounding a huge gong, and after praying for a few minutes, he places a few copper coins in large open boxes with oblique slits. Shintoism has gods and goddesses of wind, ocean, fire, food and pestilence, of mountains and rivers, certain trees, certain temples, in fact eight hundred myriads of them. The chief among them is Amaterasu, the radiant goddess of the sun, born from the left eye of Izanagi, the creator of Japan, while from his right eye the god of the moon was produced and from his nose the violent god Susa-no-o. Amaterasu was the ancestress of the line of heaven-descended mikados, who have reigned in unbroken succession from the beginning of the world, and are themselves living deities. Hence the sun goddess is honoured amongst all the rest, her shrine at Ise being the Mecca of Japan. There are no regular services in which the people take part, and only when offering the morning or evening sacrifices do the priests wear a distinct dress. The services consist in the useful presentations of rice, fish, fruit, game, vegetables, animals, etc., and in the recital of formal addresses or petitions.

There are both Shinto priests and priestesses, who need not, however, be celibate, and can give up their religious duties at any moment It is a convenient religion and suits the easy-going Japanese, whose peculiar ideas as to morality are so proverbial.

Passing through the gateway, one ascends through beautiful avenues of cryptomerias, with their dark green foliage and gigantic trunks, under which thousands of stone lanterns are placed, which are illuminated on special feast days. There are so many of these stone structures that no one knows the number. About a quarter of a mile distant the principal temple is reached, and here the ancient sacred dance of the kegura is performed every morning by girl priestesses attired in red gowns, with white aprons and their faces painted a deathly colour with white lead. On their heads were branches of artificial wistaria and a red camellia, and their hair was gathered into one long hanging tress.

After bargaining with the older priests to witness the performance for a dollar, three of the six giggling maids came forward on to the kegura platform, and immediately their faces assumed a more reverential and solemn cast. Two young priests assumed a sitting posture, one of whom commenced a weird chant, while the other played on a flute and an elderly priestess on the koto, an instrument four to five feet in length placed on the ground. Then the girls went through a slow posturing dance, holding, firstly bunches of little brass bells, and, secondly fans. When it was concluded they returned to the corner and resumed their giggling. The performance was additionally interesting, because of its having been carried on for over a thousand years. Returning in another direction through the wood we passed the temple of Tamuke-yama, celebrated in

Japanese poetry, as the scene of an ode which all Japanese know by heart. It has been roughly translated thus:—

"This time I bring with me no offerings; the gods may take to their hearts' content of the damask of the maple-leaves on Mount Tamuke."

This allusion to the maple trees is made in consequence of the large numbers of them growing round the spot. We then passed several open bazaars where sword sticks and cutlery were being made, and numbers of toys representing the sacred deer, Shinto gods, and little wooden carved figures, exquisitely painted and representing the costumes worn during a special festival, called the "No" performances, were being sold. Returning to the inn, we departed in jinrickshas, with runners, for our long ride of 27 miles on the country roads to Kyoto. Each jinricksha had an outrunner, and inclusive of stoppages for an hour for giru-hozen (lunch) the journey was accomplished in five hours, which was exceedingly good work, as the men ran up and down hill at the same speed without stopping. Luncheon we partook of at a quaint chaya, or tea house, with a miniature garden containing a little grotto, ponds of large gold fish and carp, and a few azaleas and dwarfed trees. How these trees are dwarfed and grow in the grotesque way they do passes my comprehension, but it is only part and parcel of the funny things one sees in this land of quaint conceits and preposterous fancies. In this same tea house, the same inquisitive but courteous manners were observable. As we ate, a crowd soon collected and the waitress would not leave the table alone, until we gently uttered a "mo yorushii,"—'that will do,'—which was repeated to the onlookers with astonishment. When Japanese understand anything you say to them, they can scarcely control themselves for pleasure, and give vent to Gilbertian "harmless merriment," with a vengeance.

During the last few miles of the drive, when nearing Kyoto, the roads became crowded with passengers, both walking, and riding in jinrickishas. The "three little maids from school" we constantly met, only not the counterfeit representations of the original, but real laughing ones, with the most roguish expressions and brimful of fun, and with their heads all close together and walking with their funny shuffling ways. Directly that they would see they were noticed, they placed their hands over their mouths and, in fact giggled just like they do so pleasantly at the "Savoy."

Then the babies with bright colored blue

and red dresses, and looking just like exaggerated specimens of the Japanese dolls, with the shaven heads seen in the shop windows at home. This is the paradise of babies and young children. The mothers always carry them on their backs, where they seem quite at home, but as soon as they run they are always in the roadways.

A Japanese young lady's costume is certainly the most original get-up possible. Firstly, she wears the "geta," or wooden shoes, and socks with a special receptacle for the big toe, a tightly fitting short skirt covered in front with a mairgaki or apron, and over her shoulders a loosely fitting cloak of crêpe, called a kimono, folded gracefully in front in a seme-décolleté fashion, with perhaps a little bright mauve neckerchief next the skin. The kimono has long sleeves, in which handkerchiefs of soft paper are kept to blow her small nose with, also numerous small articles, viz., her porcelain tea cup, her chop sticks, and her small visiting cards. Round her waist she wears the obi, a brightly coloured sash tied behind in a large baglike knot, not unlike the bustle formerly worn by ladies. One then comes to the head-dress, a marvellous work of art, that would do credit to a distinguished coiffeur. The hair is always raven black, shining with oil and without a crease, adorned with long white ivory pins and on special days with a red camellia. When once arranged this head-dress lasts for three or four days, and that is the reason why they use no pillows, but rest their heads on pieces of wood. It is a pretty sight to witness the courtesies and etiquette, when one of these demure young ladies calls upon another. Standing at the doorway she drops

three or four funny little curtseys, and then
steps daintily up the wooden barrier to the
raised floor where her friend meets her.
Then a formal conversation begins in
this fashion : — *Visitor*, " I am afraid I
inconvenienced you very much the other day;"
Hostess, " Not at all, your presence was most
welcome;" *Visitor*, " But I ought not to have
stayed so long, and partaken of tea;"
Hostess, " I assure you. I was delighted to
see you." After these formalities are over,
which Japanese etiquette demands, they both
sit down on the bamboo mats round the charcoal
hibacho and partake of straw-colored tea
and long red and green cakes, indulging
in the same harmless scandal that ladies
are so partial to all the world over.

But all this time we are nearing Kyoto,
and just outside the city, we pull up to
visit another enormous Dai Butsu; but this

one with only head and shoulders, though perhaps, the largest head ever cast; of the following dimensions:—

> Total height,—58 feet,
> Length of face,—30 feet,
> Breadth of face,—21 feet,
> Length of eye,—5 feet,
> Length of nose,—9 feet,
> Length of mouth,—8 feet,
> Length of ear,—12 feet.

Ascending a gallery in the temple, one can see into the interior of the image. Near by, suspended in a gaudily decorated belfry, hangs the second of the three large bells of Japan. It is 14 feet high, and weighs 63 tons. Continuing, we enter Kyoto and our coolies pull us up in fine style before the several carved wooden buildings which comprise Yaamis' hotel.

April 2nd, Easter Sunday. The hotel is situated on the slope of the hills above Kyoto, and from the windows one obtains a beautiful view of the extensive city lying below in a fertile plain, through which the river Kamogawa flows, and bounded by a range of mountains, stretching for many miles. The city contains between three to five thousand inhabitants, and is laid out with the streets all running at right angles, like Philadelphia. There are charming gardens surrounding the hotel with winding grottoes, in and out of which stand bronze storks, while cherry and plum trees just bursting into bloom, azaleas and dwarfed trees are growing. At one o'clock we were invited to witness a display of day fireworks consisting of rockets, which after explosion, disclosed, not beautiful coloured stars, but Japanese paper lanterns, birds, butterflies, parachutes, red balls, and even ladies' dresses, which expanded themselves and floated away. The hotel is also en fête, in consequence of the completion of a new wing, opened to-day by the governor of Kyoto. Large strings of red lanterns were suspended from the trees and across the houses, while at the entrance to the garden triumphal arches, decorated with camellias and branches of cherry blossom, were erected. In the evening in an adjoining tea-house, we witnessed a geisha dance. The geishas are singing girls, who perform curious posturing dances with fans, masks, parasols, and handkerchiefs, used alternately as accessories and accompanied by the tuneful samisen and a kind of drum, shaped like an hour glass, beaten with the hands. These instruments are played by other girls seated on the floor. There were about twenty in all, mostly ranging from fourteen to sixteen years of age, and dressed in coloured crêpes and silk kimonos, with the silk obi or sashes, ornamented with chrysanthemums, &c.

The samisen has no harsh sound, and is played with a piece of ivory, called a bachi. All the love songs are sung to its accompaniment, and lately an American gentleman composed one in honor of a Yokohama belle, of which the following are verses:—

"I strive to make love, but in vain, in vain,
My language I know is not plain, not plain,
 Whenever I try,
  She says, 'Gomen nasai,'
Watakshi wakaremasen, masen.*
She plays on the soft samisen, samisen,
She sings me a song now and then, and then,
 And when I go away,
  She sweetly will say,
 Sayonara! Do please come again, again."

---

* Deign honourably to excuse me, but I do not understand.

At the conclusion of the entertainment, the girls, who were then allowed to mix freely with the audience, were highly delighted at being allowed to handle and inspect specimens of jewellery worn by the English and American ladies present.

CHAPTER VIII.

KYOTO AND ITS TEMPLES—CLOISONNÉ—DESCENT OF THE RAPIDS — LAKE BIWA—ODZU—NAGOYA — FUJIAMA — YOKOHAMA— MIYANOSHITA—TOKIO — NIKKO AND ITS WONDERFUL TEMPLES—RETURN TO YOKOHAMA—DAI BUKU AT KAMAKURA.

APRIL 3rd. To-day we have visited some of the wonderful temples for which Kyoto is famous. First we proceeded to the Buddhist Chion-in, founded in 1211. A broad avenue of cherry trees leads up to a gateway, eighty one feet high, passing which the temple is seen standing in a large quadrangle. It is one of the largest wooden structures in Kyoto, 167 feet long and 94 feet from the ground. The interior is most gorgeous; old bronzes, large brass lotus flowers, thirty feet high; and gongs surrounding Buddha's golden shrine. Close by, among the trees stands the bell tower, containing The Great Bell of Japan, weighing seventy four tons. It was cast in 1633. A large piece of timber is hung at right angles, to allow the faithful to sound the bell. Proceeding from the temple we "ricksha'd" out to Nanjenji, where is another elaborately carved gateway, then on two miles further to the Ginkakuji, the principal feature of which to note, was its garden cultivated by Soami, one of Japan's greatest horticulturists. At the end of the hill stood a garden covered with azaleas. We then went to a very ancient temple called Shimogama, approached by a splendid avenue of patriarchal maple, cryptomeria, and evergreen oak trees. At the entrance, over the vermilion-painted wooden gateway are two trees, joined together by a branch that has grown from one trunk into the other. These trees are considered divine, and are much visited by women who desire to live in harmony with their husbands. Returning to the city, we visited the important monastic establishments and temples of Nishi Hong Wanji, surrounded by a broad trench. The central temple is a massive structure of the same type as are all these wooden buildings, with the copper-coloured tiled roofs. The principal gate was beautifully carved with chrysanthemum flowers and leaves. Upon exhibiting our passports we were allowed to enter a suite of state apartments, the walls of which were painted with most beautiful mural paintings, some of them 200 years old. On the way in were sliding panels decorated with peacocks and peahens on a gold background. The principal room had paintings of geese, storks, and Japanese characters and scenery. The next room was decorated with chrysanthemums and fans in the compartments of the ceilings; another with cherry trees and camellias, and another with Chinese landscapes and carvings of wistaria. In the gardens of the monastery were ponds filled with large carp and goldfish. Near this establishment are the new temples of Higashi Hong Wanji, not yet completed. A thousand men have been employed upon these for ten years, and when completed they will probably be the largest temples in Japan. Vast sums of money have been contributed in the provinces, and even peasants have contributed timber.

The length of the larger temple is 210 feet, depth 170 feet, height 120 feet, number of pillars 96 and number of tiles on roof is 163,512. We then went on to the San-ju-san-gen-do founded in 1132. This contains 1,000 images of Kwannon, the goddess of mercy. These images are ranged in tiers, as in an amphitheatre. They are all gilded, are five feet high, and form a most impressive sight. On the foreheads and round the halos are tiny gods, so that the total number of images computed to be in this wooden temple, 400 feet long, is 33,333. Kwannon is represented with about twelve hands, all issuing from wings, and no two images are alike.

We then proceeded through a long cemetery to the temples of Nishi, Otani, and to the ancient Kiyomizu-dera, built high up on the mountain side on gigantic piles. The origin of this last-named temple is lost in the midst of fable. This completed our day of visits to temples.

April 4*th*.—Rapids of the Oigawa. The descent of these rapids is one of the most exciting experiences to be obtained in Japan. In order to reach them we started on a jinricksha ride for two hours up a steep mountain road. A miniature St. Gothard tunnel pierced the top part of the pass, and we then descended for a half-hour to a high-lying upland village called Kameyama, where we lunched. Then we descended to the river, and were taken on board a kind of raft, 40 feet long, with a few planks at the sides and tapering to a point. The coolies, the jinrickshas, and eight rowers besides ourselves were conveyed with us, and we commenced the descent. The river falls through a wild mountain gorge over black boulders and rocks for seven miles; and the sensation of dashing over foaming waters in narrow channels with barely sufficient space for a vessel was exciting and novel in the extreme. A man stood in the bow holding a long bamboo, with which he dexterously steered the course of the boat between the rocks, just as it appeared that we must be hurled with the velocity of the current upon them. Down we went, over roaring cataracts and seething waters, while the boat now and then thumped unpleasantly against the rocks, and arrived at last at Arashiyama, where we mounted our jinrickshas again and were conveyed in an hour across a fertile plain to our habitat at Kyoto. It is an arduous task to pull these large boats up stream against the fierce current, but we met several of them being towed by as many as ten mules clambering amongst the rocks, while a man punted in the stream. The most exciting of the races and rapids are named, the Hut Rapid, the High Rapid, and the Shishi-no-kuchi, or Lion's Mouth.

April 5th.—To day was spent in visiting the interesting silk embroidery establishments of Nishimura, the cloisonné enamel works of Namakawa, porcelain factory of Kinkozan, and the art curio museum of Ikeda.

(It is a humiliating fact to relate, but out of our pleasant party of five, three are light weights, while the Major and I weigh about 29 stone between us, and stand over six feet in height. On emerging every morning from the hotel, the thirty or so coolie men crowd round and courteously invite the "lighter weights" to take seat in their "rickshas," while we two are left in the cold, and have to seat ourselves in the nearest vacant ones in the most ignominious manner.)

Cloisonné, or shippo, is a kind of enamel, having a very beautiful polish and colours, and the process of manufacture is a long and intricate one. First the coppersmith moulds and cuts the copper into the shape desired, then wire is fixed on the piece according to the design already drawn. The spaces between the wire are then filled in with enamel of different colours and fired. This firing process is repeated seven or eight times, and each time more enamel is filled in. After the firing is completed, the piece passes into the polishers' hands, and is then turned out as a finished specimen of cloisonné.

April 6th.—Another pleasant excursion was to Lake Biwa, lying high in the mountains and surrounded by beautiful snow-covered peaks. After two hours' ride we descended to the town of Otzu on the borders of the lake. This place has gained an unenviable notoriety through the attempted murder of the Czarewitch there on the 11th May, 1891; and some of the good people of Otzu have endeavoured to change the name of the place, but in this case the suggestion has not been adopted, although such changes are not rare in Japan. Skirting the borders of the lake we came to the hamlet of Karasaki, where is one of the most curious trees in the world, a giant pine, not famous for its height, but for its extent. It stands on an acre of ground, and the following are its dimensions:—height 90 feet, circumference of trunk 37 feet, length of branches from east to west 240 feet, from north to south 288 feet, and there are over 380 branches. Most of the branches stretch downwards, and in many cases one has to stoop to go under them. They are also so heavy that they are supported by scaffoldings of stone. From Lake Biwa a canal is made to connect the lake with Kyoto, by means of three long tunnels under the mountains, through which we were conveyed in a covered barge. The longest of these interesting water tunnels was three miles in length.

April 7th.—To day was occupied in visiting the Mikado's palace, which is now never used by His Imperial Majesty. It stands on 26 acres of ground, is only one storey high, and is surrounded by a high wall of lath and plaster, outside which, in a narrow trench about a yard in width, a stream of fresh water was flowing. The interior was unfurnished, and cold and comfortless in the extreme. After exhibiting the usual orders to view received from Tokio we were permitted to divest ourselves of our boots and to enter. The only objects of interest were some copies of the original panel paintings, in the throne room, representing Chinese sages, and beautifully painted scenes in some of the smaller audience rooms, representing chrysanthemums, wild geese, storks, etc. In the evening we witnessed a gala performance in the Japanese theatre, in honour of the advent of Spring, with its cherry and plum blossoms. The female musicians sat on raised platforms on the right and left sides of the audience, those on the right playing the samisen, and those on the left the suzumy, a kind of drum. The entertainment consisted solely of a ballet divertisement, and was in reality a glorification of spring. The three curtains represented respectively a cherry tree, a plum tree, and a giant cryptomeria. Thirty-two girls attired in most gorgeous costumes and wearing plum and cherry blossoms, went through a very characteristic dance. The first scene was the exterior of the palace, the second the throne room, and the third represented orchards of the cherry and plum trees full of the double blossoms, and illuminated with hundreds of lights. The audience was very appreciative, and behaved like a superior kind of English one.

The Japanese cherry tree is cultivated not for its fruit but for its blossom, called sakura, and is more lovely than anything Europe has to show. It holds in Japan the same position as the rose does in England.

April 8th.—Left by the Tokaido railway for Nagoya, passing en route over the Long bridge of Seta, built over an arm of Lake Biwa. This bridge has been made classic ground by a legend taken from the Japanese fairy tale series and called, "My Lord Bag of rice." Nagoya we reached in five hours. This city contains about 160,000 inhabitants. Its two grand sights are its wonderful castle and a magnificent Buddhist temple. The castle was erected in 1610 by twenty great feudal lords, but vast damage has been done recently by the great earthquake. The principal object of interest is a five storied donjon visible all over the city, on the roof of which are placed two golden dolphins eight feet high. They were made when the castle was erected in 1610, by General Kato Kiyomasco, who also built the keep. One of these dolphins was sent to the Vienna Exhibition in 1873, but on its way back it was wrecked in the Messageries Maritimes steamer, "Nil;" it was recovered however, with great difficulty, and restored to its original position much to the satisfaction of the good people of Nagoya. The grand Buddhist temple, called Higashi Hongwangi, is built like all the temples, of wood, with the handsome copper-coloured tiles for roofing. The interior was very impressive and reminded one of a most gorgeously-ornamented Roman Catholic shrine in Rome. In the centre stood a golden Buddha with uplifted hand, and round this were grouped beautifully carved lacquer wood tables, chairs, screens, faldstools and gongs, incense burners in bronze, and lotos flowers.

Nagoya presents like the other cities much the same anomalous position of semi-civilization. Broad spacious roads lined with the two-storied paper-like wooden houses, have avenues of telegraph poles along them, and are illuminated with brush electric lights. Even the little inn, with its flimsy rooms, boasted of six European bedsteads, and was lighted by electricity. There are not, even in England, many country inns that can boast of possessing the electric light, and yet we were served here with a table-d'hote of half a dozen courses, excellently cooked and served, and waited upon hand and foot by the proprietor and his courteous Japanese young ladies, who were endeavouring all they could to add to their knowledge of the English language. The inn was significantly and rightly named the "Hotel du Progrés."

April 9th.—We continued our journey at 8.20 a.m. by rail, through characteristic mountain and lake scenery, to Yokohama, which we reached in twelve hours. The principal sight of that day was a glorious view of the majestic snow-covered mountain of Fujiama, rising out of the plain to the imposing height of 12,234 feet. Though now quiescent, Fuji must still be called a volcano, because frequent mention is made in Japanese literature of the smoke of Fuji. The ascent is made from many sides, and is not difficult. The summit consists of a series of peaks surrounding the crater, about 2,000 feet in diameter. The whole Japanese nation seems, as it were, to grovel at the feet of Fuji. Their poets have sung its praises in all ages, and one in particular, who lived before the time of King Alfred, sings as follows:—

"There on the border, where the land of Kai

Doth touch the frontier of Saruga's land,

A beauteous province stretched on either hand,

See Fujiama rear his head on high!

The clouds of heaven in reverent wonder pause;

Nor may the birds those giddy heights assay,

Where melt thy snows amid thy fires away,

Or thy fierce fires lie quenched beneath thy snows.

What name might fitly tell, what accents sing

Thine awful, godlike grandeur? In thy breast

That holdeth Narusawas' flood at rest,

Thy side whence Fujikawa's waters spring.

Great Fusiyama, towering to the sky;

A treasure art thou, given to mortal man;

A god-protector, watching o'er Japan;

On thee for ever let me feast mine eye."

Fuji is depicted, with most incongruous ideas of perspective, on all the screens, fans, embroideries, tapestries, and outside shop windows, and in fact is almost deified.

Yokohama is perhaps, one of the least interesting of Japanese cities, as it is essentially a modern European settlement, around which a native town has grown. There are large hotels, tempting curio shops, bazaars, banks, post office, etc., which are uninteresting to the sightseer in Japan. One's curiosity and interest in these are soon exhausted, and so we planned an excursion to the mountain health-resort of Miyanoshita, in the lovely district of Hakone.

Here are sulphur baths, frequented by Japanese of both sexes, and innumerable bathing houses are scattered about in the tiny valleys and upland villages. The whole neighbourhood is extremely picturesque. Beautiful falling cascades, long stretches of mountain ranges, and in this month of April the sides of the hills are enlivened with the blooms of the double cherry and plum, wild azalea and japonica just budding into flower; while in the quaint miniature gardens surrounding the houses, camellias are in bloom. In one of the most beautiful stations an enterprising Japanese has erected a modern European hotel, fitted with the electric light. The hotel is largely frequented all the year round. Japanese girls, in native costumes, wait upon the guests, and with their picturesque dresses, courteous manners and polite attention to the wants of travellers, aid not a little in making one's sojourn in this hilly country enjoyable.

Leaving Miyanoshita by 'ricksha we were

conveyed down the precipitous mountain side to Yumoto, where a tramway connects with the nearest railway station of Odzu, whence we were quickly taken to Tokio, the ancient Yeddo, the present capital of Japan with a population of nearly two million people. Here we found a large hotel, the Imperial, superior to many hotels that could have been found in London twenty-five years ago, and with all modern improvements. Broad, electric-lighted streets, with avenues of trees, under which tramcars were running, give one some further idea as to the progress the Japanese are making in civilizing or rather Americanising themselves. Unfortunately this Americanisation is only ruining their natural courteous manners, and the appearance of some of the men attired in broad-patterned English tweed suits is ludicrous to behold, when compared with the quiet-looking silk kimonos worn generally. The principal sights in Tokio are the beautifully decorated Shiba temples, containing the burial places of the Shôguns, or Generalissimos. The most interesting of these is the tomb of the second Shôgun, containing the largest specimen of gold lacquer in the world, and one of the most magnificent. Parts of it are inlaid with crystals and enamels. The shrine contains only an effigy of the Shôgun and his funeral tablet, the body being beneath the pavement. As the temples more or less are of the same style and character as those described in Kyoto, being built of carved wood, highly ornamented, and surrounded by the high bronze lanterns and giant cryptomeria trees, further description of them is unnecessary.

The Uyeno park contains large numbers of the cherry trees with their double blossoms, and, when these are in full bloom, and on a holiday when the park is crowded with holiday-making Japanese, it presents a striking mass of colour. The wistaria blooms also very freely in Tokio, the flowers being forced to nearly a yard in length, and trained over lattice in tea houses.

The burial place of the Forty-seven Ronins, is also visited by most travellers, and is noteworthy, on account of their dramatic story, which is as follows :—

"THE FORTY-SEVEN RONINS.

"Asano, lord of Ako, while at Yeddo in attendance on the Shôgun, was entrusted with the carrying out of one of the greatest state ceremonies of those times—nothing less than the reception and entertainment of an envoy from the Mikado. Now Asano was not so well versed in such matters as in the duties of a warrior. Accordingly he took counsel with another nobleman, named Kira, whose vast knowledge of ceremonies and court etiquette was equalled only by the meanness of his disposition. Resenting honest Asano's neglect to fee him for the information which he had grudgingly imparted, he twitted and jeered at him for a country lout, unworthy the name of Daïmyo. At last, he actually went so far as to order Asano to bend down and fasten up his footgear for him. Asano, long suffering though he was, could not brook such an insult. Drawing his sword, he slashed the insolent wretch in the face, and would have made an end of him, had he not sought safety in flight. The palace—for this scene took place within the precincts of the palace—was of course soon in an uproar. Thus to degrade its majesty by a private brawl was a crime punishable with death and confiscation. Asano was condemned to perform harakiri that very evening, his castle was forfeited, his family declared extinct, and all the members of his clan disbanded; in Japanese parlance they became ronins, literally "wave-men," that is, wanderers, fellows without a lord, and without a home. This was in the month of April, 1701.

So for the first Act. Act two, is "The Vengeance." " Oishe Kuranosuke, the senior retainer of the dead Daimyo, determines to avenge him, and consults with forty-six others of his most trusty fellow-lieges as to the ways and means. All are willing to lay down their lives in the attempt. The difficulty is to elude the vigilance of the Government." For, mark one curious point; the vendetta, though imperatively prescribed by custom, was forbidden by law, somewhat as duelling now is in certain western countries. Not to take vengeance on an enemy involved social ostracism. On the other hand, to take it involved capital punishment. But not to take vengeance never entered the head of any chivalrous Japanese.

"After many secret consultations, it was determined among the Ronins that they should separate and dissemble. Several of them took to plying trades. They became carpenters, smiths and merchants in various cities, by which means some of their number gained access to Kira's mansion, and learnt many of the intricacies of its corridors and gardens. Oishi himself, the head of the faithful band, went to Kyoto, where he plunged into a course of drunkenness and debauchery. He even discarded his wife and children, and took a harlot to live with him. Thus was their enemy, to whom full reports of all these doings were brought by spies, lulled to complete security at last. Then suddenly, on the night of the 30th January, 1703, during a violent snow-storm, the attack was made. The forty-seven Ronins forced the gate of Kira's mansion, slew his retainers and dragged forth the high-born, but chicken-hearted wretch from an outhouse, in which he had sought to hide himself behind a lot of firewood and charcoal. Respectfully, as befits a mere gentleman when addressing a great noble, the leader of the band requested Kira to perform harakiri, thus giving him a chance of dying by his own hand, and so saving his honour. But Kira was afraid, and there was nothing for it but to kill him, being the scoundrel that he was.

"That done, the little band formed in order, and marched (day having now dawned), to the temple of Ginkakuji, at the other end of the city. On their way thither, the people all flocked out to praise this doughty deed; a great Daïmyo, whose palace they passed, sent out refreshments to them with messages of sympathy, and at the temple they were received by the abbot in person. There they laid on their lord's grave, which stood in the temple grounds, the head of the enemy by whom he had been so grievously wronged. Then came the official sentence, condemning them all to commit harakiri. This they did separately, in the mansions of the various Daïmyos, to whose care they had been entrusted for the last few days of their lives, and then they also were buried in the same temple grounds, where their tombs can be seen to this day."

The enthusiastic admiration of a whole people during two centuries has been the reward of their obedience to the ethical code of their time and country.

Leaving Tokio by the Nikko branch line, we proceeded in five hours to the village of Hachi-ishi, close to which are the most celebrated mausolea in Japan, called the temples of Nikko. These consist of the tombs of the first and third Shôguns, Ieyasa and Iemitsu. For a considerable distance alongside the railway line ran a portion of one of the greatest monuments of Japan, viz.: an avenue of giant cryptomeria trees, which is supposed to extend for 300 miles across the country from Kobe to Nikko, and under which processions of pilgrims wend their way to worship at the temples of Nikko. The village is situated high up in the mountains, at an altitude of 1,780 feet above sea level, and consists of a street of the usual wooden houses with tiled roofs, stretching for nearly two miles up hill. Arrived at the summit, we turned sharp round a corner and came immediately in sight of the sacred bridge spanning the river Daigawa, which here runs through a picturesque ravine, while mountains hem in the valley on all sides. This bridge was built in 1638, is painted entirely vermilion colour, and is only opened for pilgrims to pass over twice a year. It is supported on enormous solid piers of stone, and is 84 feet long. Unquestionably these beautifully decorated temples and gateways surrounding the tombs of these celebrated Shôguns, are the principal sights of Japan, and merit a lengthy description. The first temple we visited was that of Jemitsu. At the principal gate was a gigantic pair of wooden figures;

passing through this gate we entered an open court, surrounded by carved wooden buildings, and ascended a stone staircase to the gate called Niten-mon, containing colossal figures, one painted red and the other green, of Bishamon and Ida-ten, who are mythological protectors of Buddhism. The inside niches of the gate were occupied by the gods of wind and of thunder. Three more flights of stone steps brought us to the demon gate, from which a glorious view of the dark green foliage and surrounding pine-covered hills was obtained. Passing through this and taking off our boots, we were permitted to enter the oratory and chapel, which were filled with the usual gorgeous decorations and insignia attached to the Buddhist religion. The tomb itself is situated in the open air, higher up the mountain side, and is entirely of bronze. In front of it stood a gate of bronze, covered with Sanscrit characters in shining brass. The mausoleum of Ieyasu, the most celebrated of the Shôguns, is surrounded by picturesque groupings of wonderfully carved buildings, bearing representations of peonies, chrysanthemums, tigers, tapirs, monkeys, elephants, etc., all painted in bright red and blue colours. Three of these buildings are very handsome, and are used as storehouses, in which utensils employed in the religious ceremonies performed in honour of Ieyasu, also pictures, furniture, etc., used by him during his lifetime, are preserved. A very interesting object is the On Chozuya, containing a holy-water cistern made of a solid piece of granite, erected in 1618. On the roof are painted dragons.

Ascending a flight of steps, we passed into another courtyard, just outside which are two stone lions in the act of leaping down; and these were given by Iemitsu. On the right side of this court stood a bell tower, a bronze candelabrum given by the king of Loo-choo, and a bell given by the king of Korea, called the moth-eaten bell, because of there being a hole just under the ring by which the bell is suspended. On the left stood a bronze lantern from Korea, a candelabrum from Holland, a drum tower, and behind these a temple dedicated to the Buddhist god Yakushi-Nyorai. In this court were no fewer than 118 bronze lanterns, standing in rows, each about eight feet high, given by various Daimyos, and adorned with the three-leaved crest of the Shôgun in brass. Ascending from this court by another flight of steps we arrived at the platform, on which stands the most exquisitely carved wooden gate in Japan, called the

Yo-mei-mon. The following description is well narrated, by Murray :—

"The columns supporting it are carved with a minute geometrical pattern and painted white. The pillar next beyond has the pattern carved upside down, which was done purposely, lest the flawless perfection of the whole structure should bring misfortune on the house of Tokergawa, by exciting the jealousy of heaven. It is called the Ma-yoke-no-Hashira, or evil-averting pillar. The side niches are lined with a pattern of graceful arabesques founded upon the peony; those on the outside contain the images called Sadaijan and Udaijin, armed with bows and carrying quivers full of arrows at their backs; the inner niches have Ama'inu and Komainu. The capitals of the columns are formed of unicorns' heads. The architrave of the second story is adorned with white dragons' heads where the cross beams intersect, and in the centre of each side and end is a magnificently involved dragon with golden claws. Above the architrave of the lower story projects a balcony which runs all round the building. The railing is formed of children at play, while below it are groups of Chinese sages and immortals. Gilt dragons' heads with gaping crimson throats support the roof, and from the top a demon looks down."

Passing under this wonderful gateway we entered another court, enclosed on three sides by a cloister. On the right side were two buildings, one of which contained a stage upon which a very old Shinto priestess, with blackened teeth was sitting, who, at our approach, went through the sacred dance of the Kegura again; in the other building, are preserved the cars carried in procession on the 1st June, when the deified spirits of Ieyasu, Hideyoski, and Yoritomo, are supposed to occupy them. In the centre of this inner court, surrounded by a fence, stood the oratory and chapel. The folding doors of the former are lavishly decorated with arabesques of peonies in gilt relief.

Over the door and windows are five compartments filled with birds, carved in relief, four on each side of the building. The interior is a large matted room, 42 feet long by 27 feet wide, with an ante-chamber at each end. That on the right, which was intended for the Shôgun, contains pictures of unicorns on a gold ground, and four carved oak panels of phœnixes. The rear compartment of the building is of carved wood, with the Tokugawa crest in the centre, surrounded by phœnixes and chrysanthemums. The opposite ante-chamber has the same number of panels, the subjects of which are eagles, and a carved and painted ceiling with an angel surrounded by chrysanthemums. The gold paper, "gohei," at the back of the oratory, and a circular mirror, were the only ornaments left, the Buddhist paraphernalia of bells, gongs, prayer books. lotus flowers, incense burners, etc., having been removed when the Shinto form of worship was introduced. To reach Ieyasu's tomb, after leaving the beautiful oratory, one ascends a moss grown gallery and several steep flights, about 200 steps altogether, up the hill behind, to a paved courtyard, in the centre of which stands the tomb, shaped like a small pagoda. It is made of a single bronze casting of a light colour, produced by the admixture of gold. In front stood a low stone table, bearing an immense bronze stork, with a brass candle in its mouth, an incense burner of bronze, and a vase with artificial lotos, flowers and leaves in brass. The whole is surrounded by a balustrade; the entrance to the enclosure, being by a large bronze gate, not exposed to the open. The whole tomb is very impressive; and surrounded as these temples are, by magnificent cedars and cryptomerias, the whole neighbourhood is singularly appropriate for purposes of worship. The sights in Nikko are legion, but are of minor interest compared with the above-mentioned temples. Outside the enclosure of Ieyasu's tomb stands a graceful five-storied pagoda, painted mostly of vermilion, and built in 1650. It is 104 feet high. Round the lower story are life-like painted carvings of the twelve signs of the Zodiac. Not far from this stands the Buddhistic monastery of Mangwangi, the principal hall of which is called the hall of the three Buddhas, viz :—the thousand-handed Kwannon, the horse-headed Kwannon, and Amida Nyorai. The whole neighbourhood is suitable for a prolonged visit, as there are mountains to climb, picturesque mountain lakes, falling cascades, and brawling rivers to explore, combined with other interesting temples and villages. The air is more bracing, than in the neighbourhood of the large towns situated in the lowlands, and surrounded by the plains of the irrigated rice fields.

Leaving picturesque Nikko we returned to Tokio, where we spent another day; and then took train to Yokohama, visiting *en route* Kamakura, famous for its giant Dai Butsu, or open air bronze statue of Buddha, which stands in a miniature valley and is of the following dimensions:—

Height,—49 feet, 7 inches.
Circumference,—97 feet, 2 inches.
Length of face,—8 feet, 5 inches.
Width from ear to ear,—17 feet, 9 inches.
Length of eye,—3 feet, 11 inches.
Length of eyebrow,—4 feet, 2 inches.
Length of ear,—6 feet, 6 inches.
Length of nose,—3 feet, 9 inches.

Width of mouth,—3 feet, 2 inches.

Curls, of which there are 830,—each 9 inches.

Length from knee to knee,—35 feet, 8 inches.

The eyes are of pure gold, and the image was formed of sheets of bronze, cast separately, brazed together, and finished off with the chisel. The hollow interior of the image contains a small shrine, and the visitor may ascend into the head.

The statue stands alone among Japanese works of art. " No other gives such an impression of majesty, or so truly symbolises the central figure of Buddhism. The intellectual calm which comes of perfected knowledge and the subjugation of all passion. To be fully appreciated it must be visited several times."

CHAPTER IX.

JAPANESE LITERATURE—ENGLISH, AS IT IS JAPPED—
OPTIMISTIC AND PESSIMISTIC VIEWS OF JAPAN—THE
SANDWICH ISLANDS—THE VOLCANO KILAUEA.

JAPAN has interested us more than any other land yet visited, and six months would not be too long a stay in this delightful country to see its sights, to appreciate fully the beauties of the country, and to understand the customs of its inhabitants.

Its language is very harmonious and sweet, but almost impossible to read, as the Chinese characters are used. However, English is spoken very extensively in all the principal cities, and the principal bazaars and shops exhibit signs in Japanese with English translations, some of which are very ludicrous because of the mistakes in spelling, etc. In fact, English, as she is Japped, forms quite an interesting study; and I append a few specimens :—

"The improved milk."
"The European monkey jacket make for the Japanese."
"Carver and Gilder for sale."
"Draper, milliner and ladies' outfatter."
"The ribbons, the laces, the veils and the feelings.*"

"NOTIES.

"Our tooth is a very important organ for human life and countenance as you know; therefore, when it is attack by disease or injury, artificial tooth is also very useful."

"I am engage to the Dentistry and I will make for your purpose."

---

* Frillings.

Japanese are very fond of entering into correspondence with Englishmen, in order to improve their knowledge of the language, and the following are amusing letters:—

"TOKYO, *January 1st*, 1890.
"Dear Sir,

"New Year very happy. I salute you prudently for you all. I had been several districts since July of last year. Now, here my head is mingled up with several admirations by the first voyage to abroad; but anyhow I feel very lionizing, interesting, profitable for experiment, by sailing about there and here. Though I excercised English diligently, yet I'm very clumsiness for translation, dialogue, composition, elocution and all other. It is a great shamefulness really, but I don't abandon English henceforth and I swear to learn it perseveringly, even if in the lucubration.

"Tendering you my sympathetic joy of your decoration.

"I am

"Yours affectionately

"M. TSUDA."

"SAGA, *August* 18*th*.

'ROBERT FANSHAW, ESQ.

" G. B. Consul.

" Dear Sir,

"I am very glad to hear that you and your family are very well and I am also quite well as usual, but my grandfather's disease is very severe without changing as customary. I fear that it is a long time since I have pay a visit to you. I wish your pardon to get away my remote crime. We have only a few hot in Saga, as well as summer is over, and we feel to be very cool in morning and evening. Sometimes we have an earthquake here at now, but the mens was afright no more. I grieves that a terrible accident took place in the school of Military Saga. The story of it, a scholar had put to death some colleague with a greate stick on the floor, and a Doctor of Anatomy dissected immediately with dead disciple, then all pupils of school were now to question its matter in the judgement seat; but do not it decide yet.

" Unequivocal matter would speak you of kind letter.

" I am, &c.,

" K. TANAKA."

England, having been set as a theme in a school in Tokyo, the following essay was composed by one of the pupils:—

"The England which occupied of the largest and greatest dominion which rarely can be. The Englishman works with a very powerful hands and the long legs and even the eminenced mind, his chin is so strong as decerved iron. He are not allowed it to escape if he did seize something. Being spread his dominion is dreadfully extensive, so that his countrymen boastally say "the sun are never sets on our dominions." The Testamony of English said, that he that lost the common sense, he never any benefit though he had gained the whole world. The English are cunning institutioned to established a great Empire of the Paradise. The Englishman always said to the other nation "Give me your land and I will give you my Testamony." So it is not a robber but exchanged, as the Englishman always confide the object to be pure, and the order to be holy, and they reproach him, if any them are killed to death, with the contention of other man."

An Optimistic View of Japan.

The following lines were written with the moonlight shining full upon the Bay of Tokio, after a good dinner at the Grand hotel. The writer, Dr. William Hellmuth, of New York, had just returned from a delightful excursion to Kamakura, on a beautiful day in July.

I.

"Oh, fair Japan! oh, rare Japan!
Thou land of ancient trees,
Where lotos blossoms fringe thy paths,
And perfume every breeze.
Where lilies bend their fragrant heads
To kiss thy plashing streams,
And dark skinned musumés,—almond-eyed,—
Wake long forgotten dreams.

2.

"Thy hills crown-capped with sacred groves,

Enclose thy gilded shrines,

In grottoes where the iris blooms,

Droop sweet wistaria vines.

Mysterious languor seems to hang

O'er mountain, plain and rill:

An unreality of life

Does all the senses fill.

3.

"Thine ancient shrines to Buddha blest,

With Shintos' gilded spires,

Proclaim a soul-sustaining rest,

And ecstasy inspires.

Oh! sweet it is to dwell with thee,

" Land of the Rising sun,"

Where beauty, age and mystery

Combine themselves in one."

A Pessimistic View of Japan.

These verses were also composed by Dr. Hellmuth, while lying in bed at Miyanoshita, during the drying of his clothes in the kitchen, after a five hours' exposure in a hurricane of rain and wind (a portion of the typhoon of Japan), over one of the highest passes in Japan, Otomotge. Discouraged, cold, drenched to the skin, shrivelled and dispirited, he came to Fujiya hotel and thought in his misery :—

I.

"Oh, hang Japan! oh, dang Japan!
A land of gnats and fleas;
Where noisome odours fill the air
And float on every breeze.
Where men run naked in the streets,
Wear spectacles for clothes;
And old and young, and rich and poor
Eschew the use of hose.

2.

"Oh, land devoid of knives and forks,
Of tables, chair and beds:
Where women black their teeth, and shave
Their little babies' heads.
I've had enough, I have no use
(A quiet New York man)
For all this rude simplicity,
Careering round Japan.

3.

" I've had enough of cloisonné,
Of ivory carvings, too,
Of ancient rare Satsuma jugs,
Which probably are new.
I hate the sight of Buddha fat,
He's too infernal calm ;
And temples, shrines and lacquer ware
And daimios, I ? ? ? "hem"—

4.

"Boy, bring my clothes up from the wash
As quickly as you can;
Sir Edwin Arnold writes a lot
Of bosh about Japan.
I'm shivering cold, I'm wringing wet;
I've been an idle dreamer!
To Yokohama let me get,
And there, thank Heaven! a steamer."

April 29*th*. We embarked on board the Occidental and Oceanic Company's Steamship "Oceanic," lying in Yokohama harbour, and sailing down Mississipi bay, we were rolling in the Pacific ocean, with a stiff north-easterly breeze blowing.

May 6*th*. During the night we passed the Midway islands. In travelling westward we gained a day, while vessels proceeding eastwards lose one, so we have just experienced the novelty of spending two

May the fifths. This is our eighth day of perpetual rolling, and every one is looking forward hopefully to our arrival in the Sandwich Islands, which we hope to reach on Tuesday the 9th. Not one ship, or other sign of life have we seen, with the exception of that on board our vessel, but here one has the feeling of being in a small kingdom of one's own. Cricket, quoits, shuffleboard, bezique, poker, singing, reading, and the daily sweepstake as to the run of the vessel, are our daily distractions. We have now accomplished 2,500 miles from Yokohama, being a daily average of 315 across the ocean. There are 615 persons on board, the larger number of whom are Chinamen proceeding to San Francisco. Before a Chinaman will proceed on an ocean voyage, a stipulation is entered into between him and the Steamship Company, that in the event of his death occuring during the voyage his body will be embalmed by the ship's doctor, placed in a coffin and returned to the Celestial Empire. Large numbers of curiously shaped coffins, are carried therefore by the steamers, and we have noticed since leaving Yokohama that one of the two rows of coffins has disappeared.

May 9th.—This morning at ten o'clock the mountains of Oahu, one of the Sandwich islands, distant 3,400 miles from Yokohama, came into view ; at 11.30 we were running along the coast, and soon the spires of Honolulu came into view, as well as the masts of the ships in the artificial harbour. At twelve o'clock a small steamboat, named the "Annie," came alongside, carrying the flag of the Provisional Government, and conveying the pilot and quarantine officers on board. An inspection of all the passengers who desired to go on shore was then made by the latter gentlemen, on the upper deck.

The harbour bar has been deepened during the last two years to 30 feet to enable ocean steamers to pass between the coral reefs, over which the surf is always rolling into the calm waters beyond, and great excitement was taking place on shore, as our vessel was the first to enter the harbour since the completion of the work. The total cost has been 170,000 dollars. In the harbour were, an English sloop, the "Hyacinth;" two American men of war, the "Charleston," and "Boston;" and a Japanese ship. Our ship draws 25 feet of water, and we steam slowly across the bar and right up to the wharf, where the inhabitants are thronging to witness a vessel of our tonnage being moored alongside for the first time. Just as the thick hawser from our bow was tightening it broke with the report of a cannon, but this was soon repaired and we were at anchor, speedily on shore, and being driven to the Royal Hawaiian hotel. America's influence is very great, and the star-spangled banner was hanging in front of the shops and from the houses of most of the American residents. In fact, the whole town gives one the impression of being within an easy distance of the United States. American bars and saloons abound, and the gold dollar is the accepted coinage of the place.

The march of civilization has indeed made great strides, for we find on this island, in the centre of the largest piece of water in the world, and the farthest away from any great continent, broad wide streets and avenues, with the electric light suspended everywhere, tramcars running, telephones in use, natives riding safety bicycles, and ladies actually riding cross-saddle. A party of ten fellow passengers combined together, and engaged a coach and four horses from the hotel, and we were soon bowling along the good roads, and enjoying tropical scenes and vegetation again. Plantations of melons, mangoes, bananas, pretty bungalows surrounded with lovely gardens filled with crotons, hibiscus, aristologia, stephanotis, etc., and shaded by cocoanut palms, were passed. We then ascended a zigzag road to the summit of the Punch Bowl, a projecting spur of the high mountain range in the interior. On the right, a glorious view of Honolulu from this point of vantage was obtained, embosomed in beautiful fresh green.

To the left stood the bold brown bluff of Diamond Head, with the village and bathing place of Waikiki at its feet, while the ocean which we had just traversed for eleven days, seemed to stretch itself into illimitable space.

We descended to Waikiki, passed the racecourse, and were shown an ostrich farm, with 60 handsome birds; then to the queen's palace, a fine square stuccoed building, which the queen has been obliged to vacate since her dethronement. Opposite to this was the Governmental building with the Hawaiian flag flying. In the open square in front stood a bronze statue of Kamehameha I., the first king of the United Hawaiian islands, who commenced to reign in 1782 and died in 1817, at the age of 81, after 35 years' reign.

The natives are Kanakas, and very similar in type to the Maoris of New Zealand. The men are notable for height and remarkable physique, and the women are also of great size

The population of the islands is, however, very mixed, and the natives are decreasing yearly. The total population is 89,990, according to the census of 1890, and composed of different nationalities as follows :—Natives 34,436, half castes 6,186, Hawaiian born foreigners 7,495, Americans 1,928, British 1,344, German 1,034, French 70, Portuguese 8,602, Norwegians 227, Chinese 15,301, Japanese 12,360, Polynesians 588, and other nationalities 419. From the Government house we were shown the present villa residence of the dethroned queen, Liliokalani, and after a drive through the inevitable Chinatown we returned to the hotel. In the evening, the band of the provisional Government, under the conductorship of a German bandmaster, played a selection of operatic music, in a kiosk, illuminated with coloured electric lights. Afterwards we witnessed a characteristic native dance, performed by Hula Hula girls, whose dresses were mostly composed of grasses and garlands of flowers, and accompanied by harmonious rhythmical music, played on a native guitar.

Hawaii, the largest island of the group, is two days distant from Oahu, and upon this island the celebrated volcano of Kilauea is situated. This is the largest in the world, and its crater has been aptly called the Inferno, while the Hawaiian islands themselves are designated Paradise. Kilauea is the most active volcano in the world, and is situated at an elevation of 4,000 feet, on the southern slopes of Mauna Loa, one of the highest mountains in Hawaii (13,675 feet).

A visit to it necessitates a stay of at least a fortnight in the islands, with a probability of not getting berths in a steamer for a month, so we could not afford the time to visit it. Miss Bird has written the following graphic description of its appearance:—

"Suddenly, just above, and in front of us, gory

drops were tossed in air, and springing forward we stood on the brink of Hale-man-man, which was about thirty-five feet below us. We were all speechless, for a new glory and terror had been added to the earth. It is the most unutterable of all wonderful things. It is unimaginable, indescribable, a sight to remember for ever; a sight which at once took possession of every faculty of sense and soul, removing one altogether out of the range of ordinary life. Here is the real " bottomless pit," the fire which is not quenched; the lake which burneth with fire and brimstone," the fiery sea whose waves are never weary. The inner lake, while we stood there, formed a sort of crater within itself; the whole lava sea rose about three feet, a blowing cone about eight feet high was formed, and it was never the same two minutes together. And what we saw had no existence a month ago, and probably will be changed in every essential feature a month hence. What we did see was one irregularly-shaped lake, possibly 500 feet wide at its narrowest part, and nearly half a mile at its broadest, almost divided in two by a low bank of lava, which extended across it where it was narrowest, and which was raised visibly before our eyes. The surface of the double lake was continually skimming over for a second or two with a cooled crust of a luscious grey white, like frosted silver, broken by jagged cracks of a bright rose colour. The movement was nearly always from the sides to the centre, but the movement of the centre itself appeared independent, and always took a southerly direction. Before each outburst of agitation there was much hissing, and a throbbing internal roaring, as of imprisoned gases. Now it seemed furious, demoniacal, as if no power on earth could bind it; then playful and sportive, then for a second, languid; but only because it was accumulating fresh force. On our arrival, eleven fire fountains were playing joyously round the lakes; and sometimes, the six of the nearer lakes ran together in the centre, to go wallowing down in one vortex, from which they re-appear bulging upwards, till they formed a huge cone thirty feet high, which plunged downwards in a whirlpool, only to re-appear in exactly the previous number of fountains, in different parts of the lake, high leaping, raging, flinging themselves upwards. It was all confusion, commotion, force, terror, majesty, mystery, and even beauty. And the colour! "Eye hath not seen it." Molten metal has not that crimson gleam, nor blood that living light. Had I not seen this, I should never have known that such a colour was possible."

> "Hawai-nei! Of many, one thou art,
> Each scattered fragment an essential part.
>
> No jewelled setting is more fair than thee,
> O emerald cluster in a beryl sea!
>
> Thy life is music,—fate, thy notes prolong;
> Each isle a stanza; and the whole, a song."
>
> G. W. STEWART.

The group of the Sandwich Islands is made up of eight inhabited islands, the most important of which are Hawaii, Oahu, Maui, Kauai, and Molokai (the leper settlement). The climate is the most delicious in the world, neither too hot nor too cold, being in the tropics, but only just over the line. Mark Twain once said of the Hawaiian islands —" No alien land in all the world has any deep, strong charm for me, but that one ; no other land could so longingly and beseechingly haunt me, sleeping and waking through half a lifetime, as that has done. Other things leave me, but it abides ; other things change, but it remains the same. For me its balmy airs are always blowing, its summer seas flashing in the sun ; the pulsing of its surf-beat is in my ear ; I can see its garlanded crags, its leaping cascades, its plumy palms drowsing by the shore; its remote summits floating like islands above the cloud racks; I can feel the spirit of its woodland solitude ; I can hear the plash of its brooks; in my nostrils still lives the breath of flowers that perished twenty years ago."

CHAPTER X.

OFF TO SAN FRANCISCO—THE YOSEMITE VALLEY—SALT LAKE CITY — CHICAGO AND THE WORLD'S FAIR — NEW YORK—DEPARTURE FOR ENGLAND.

AY 12*th*.—With an addition of new passengers, we departed at ten o'clock on our voyage to San Francisco. On the jetty the band played suitable farewell airs, such as Auld Lang Syne, the Star Spangled Banner, God Save the Queen, and the Watch on the Rhine, etc. Rounding the Diamond Head, we sailed by the side of mountains with volcanic formations; and with Molokai, the leper island on the right; while in a few hours the whole group of the Sandwich Islands had disappeared from view.

May 14*th*.—Our third day at sea. The weather is glorious. There is a light wind which sends a delicious coolness into our cabins. The ocean is a beautiful blue, and has a gentle swell. The "Oceanic," however, is by no means a steady vessel, and rolls to and fro, with a perpetual see-sawing motion, that acts as a constant lullaby, and sends us very easily to sleep. Now and then she makes a deep lurch, making all the glasses jingle and plates dance.

May 19*th*.—Off San Francisco. We have been sailing across the Pacific for seven days, without anything especially worthy of recording. When two days distant from land we noticed one sailing vessel, the only one seen during our long ocean trip.

Just before midnight last evening, we saw

the lights (the electric ones) of San Francisco gleaming, and we are now anchored close to the jetty; and America, the "land of the free and the home of the brave," is before us. We entered through its Golden Gate, "which is a narrow channel of water, guarded by two precipitous cliffs," stretching out from the hills on either side. The water inside this natural barrier broadens into a noble bay, on the right side of which lies San Francisco. Opposite are the neighbouring suburban cities of Oaklands, Alameda and Berkley; while behind them rises an amphitheatre of hills, sweeping right round the bay.

We were soon on shore, undergoing the rigorous custom-house examination, enforced by the exacting and obnoxious provisions of the Mackinley Tariff Bill. The duties levied on silk, curios, etc., are enormous. Ivory 45 per cent., unmounted photographs 40 per cent., silk 60 per cent. Having ourselves nothing dutiable, we managed to get our luggage "checked" in an hour and a half, and handed to the Transfer Company for conveyance, while we ourselves were soon taken, in a wild-west sort of coach, to the Palace hotel. All the roads are paved unevenly with cobble stones, so unless it is unavoidable, everybody rides in the electric or cable cars, which are to be found in every street. The service of these is admirable. In the principal thoroughfare there are no fewer than four sets of lines laid down, and processions of both open and closed cars are seen going constantly in all directions. There is no bustle or excitement, but everything seems to go on like clockwork, or like a piece of machinery. Somebody touches a button, and this sets the city in motion. The streets have fearful gradients, but the cars glide up and down these like exaggerated switchback railways. The city is quite cosmopolitian in appearance. Colossal blocks of buildings, intersected at right angles with broad noble arteries of great length, and covered with miles of telegraph wires and procession of the necessary poles, fill up the perspective. The market street is a most noble artery. Jumping on to a car, we ride for a few miles up and down hill, past pretty villas, built entirely of wood, in the gardens of which the most beautiful "Gloire de dijon" roses are growing, until we reach the Golden Gate park of 1,000 acres in extent. Here we found roses, fuschias, geraniums, cinerarias, rhododendrons, azaleas, the white hawthorn, and other flowers, all in full bloom, a wealth of blossom. The park is undulating, with broad carriage road; and possesses hothouses, a buffalo and deer park and aviaries. From the park another car took us across some sandy hills to the Cliff house, on the shores of the Pacific Ocean. Here are situated some wonderful rocks, a few yards out in the water, and covered with hundreds of seals and sea lions, which were basking and lying about with their brown coats in the sun. The surf along the whole coast line was very grand, viewed from this point. We returned to the city by a small railroad skirting the tops of the cliffs, giving a beautiful view of the narrow Golden Gate, and the waters of the bay beyond.

May 20*th.*—Large ferry boats capable of holding a thousand people, and worked by propellers, are used as a means of communication between San Francisco and Oaklands. Crossing in one of these to a long railway pier, built out into the shallow water, long trains take the passengers on into the city. These trains are composed of the usual Pullman cars with continuous passages; they are drawn by engines with cowcatchers in front, and they run right through the principal streets of the city.

Half-way along the back of the engine hangs a large bell, the size of an ordinary church one, which is continually rung as the train passes down the centre of the street.

The noise made by this bell is very doleful, but it effectually warns tbe populace of the approach of a train. In consequence of the permissive right acquired by the Central Pacific Railway Company, to run these trains from the harbour to their depôt through the town itself, the inhabitants possess the privilege of using the cars without payment, as long as the train is passing through the precincts of the city.

California seems a land flowing with milk and honey, It has a charming and beautiful climate, where everything grows and blooms in abundance, and here in Oaklands the pretty houses of the wealthy San Francisco merchants are surrounded with gardens containing most glorious and exquisite "Gloire de dijon" and other roses. The streets are just the same as those in the sister city; the cars to suit the convenience of the general public running down the centre of the roads, flanked right and left by hideous telegraph poles, ruining their otherwise handsome perspectives.

May 21*st.*—China Town, situated in the heart of the city, is, I am afraid a vexed question with the inhabitants of San Francisco. Here, in the centre of this brilliant capital of the west, with the ultra improvements of this go-a-head age, is a bit of China again, with its dirt and squalor, and subterranean dens, into which one is invited to penetrate by importunate guides. There it is, and there apparently it must remain, but it is a blot upon this handsome city.

May 22nd.—At four o'clock we departed for the Yosemite Valley, situated in the Sierra Nevada range of mountains. Travelling in a Pullman sleeping car for several hours we arrived at a place called Berenda, when we were switched on to a side line, where we reposed for the night.

Very early in the morning we were taken further by train a short distance, and then mounted a four-horse coach for a long two days' drive, to explore the wonders of this valley, one of America's biggest sights.

We soon commenced to mount the foothills of the Sierra Nevada range, and by noon reached a ranch called Ahwani, where we obtained lunch. With a fresh relay of horses we gradually ascended until Mount Raymond came into view, with snow covering its summit. The beautiful valleys around us were covered with yellow giant pines, wild horse chestnuts and lilacs, while beds of wild lupins made the roadside gay with their deep blue colour.

We attained an altitude of over 6,000 feet after driving a distance altogether of about twenty five miles, and thereupon descended in a zigzag manner for several miles through a pine forest to the upland valley of Wawona, where we slept. At six o'clock the following morning we were off again through the National Park of the Yosemite, to reach the famous valley. The road led continually upwards through the giant pine trees, and affording far-reaching glimpses of vast rugged mountain ranges, until turning sharply round a corner we came upon Inspiration Point, and the Yosemite valley lay beneath and before us.

We seemed quite close to it and yet we were four miles above the floor of this wonderful valley cut in the mountains. The Bridal Veil waterfall we could see dropping gently for 900 feet, over a cliff; above it rose the twin peaks of the Cathedral Spires, then came the Sentinel Rock, opposite the Capitan, while closing in the view towered the rounded peaks of the North Dome and Half Dome. We quickly accomplished the four mile descent to the bottom of the valley, and were soon right under the Bridal Veil, dropping like a piece of feathery muslin or silk, and sending up a cloud of white steam, upon which beautiful prismatic hues were reflected. The mountains reared their giant heads almost vertically around us. Stupendous masses of rock towered to the skies, all with peculiar formations, and which have received quaint names from the Indians. The Tu-si-ak (goddess of the mountains), represents the North Dome, rising like the dome of a cathedral to 8,823 feet; directly opposite to this is the To-co-yai, or Shade to Indian baby basket. Further up the valley is the Mahta (martyr mountain), or lap of liberty, Tu-tock-a-nu-la (great chief of the valley). Pom-pom-pa-sus (falling rocks), called by the Americans, the Three Brothers, etc. Between the Sentinel and the North Dome, falls drop into the valley in three parts; the Yosemite, which is the biggest drop in the world, being 2,548 feet in length.

These falls are set in a frame of such vastness and grandeur that one can scarcely imagine their true size. The waters thunder down into a chasm, foaming and churning, and throwing up volumes of white and clouded spray, which is wafted about by the wind, while a battle rages on in this seething cauldron, causing reports like cannon shots to be heard.

The width of the fall as it slips over the summit of the cliff is over 40 feet, and it is a day's journey up a trail to the summit. There are three distinct leaps, the final one dropping 1,502 feet; the water then runs down a narrow gorge, called the middle fall, for 559 feet, and then decends with a final plunge of 487 feet into the above-mentioned hidden chasm; from which the waters emerge, and mingle with the blue, placid river flowing through the centre of the valley, overshadowed by the giant pines, which raise their graceful heads out from the fallen boulders strewn about in wild confusion. Further up the river, there is another waterfall of 617 feet, called the Vernal, or Cataract of Diamonds.

The star-spangled banner waves from the summit of Glacier Point, up which an old Indian trail ascends in steep zigzags. At this point a large massive rock projects right over the precipice, upon which one can safely stand. The whole range of the Sierras can be seen from here, a wavy expanse of pine and snow-covered mountains.

In this wonderful forest, sixty miles of which we have traversed during two days, a great many of the pines rise to a height of 300 feet, while the average is about 250 feet.

Forest fires burn and scorch a great many of them, and this is very easily accomplished, as a canary-colored lichen or moss grows on the bark, and burns like tinder.

A match set to this lichen will scorch a beautiful tree in a few minutes, and leave it a blackened and scarred trunk.

Wild boar, lynx, deer, skunk and rattlesnakes abound in these regions, but we saw only a few deer; and a skunk running in front of the leaders' legs, as we were approaching Wawona. Californian quail were running about in pairs, while the work of the woodpeckers could be seen on every side, in the riddled appearance of large numbers of the trees.

The most dainty little bird we observed was the golden auriole, about the size of a canary, with a yellow breast, black wings, red beak and blue head.

On the return journey, we drove four miles out of the main road to visit the famous giant trees of Mariposa, the largest of which is named the Grizzly Giant; this mighty monarch is over 800 feet high and 38 feet in circumference. There are over one hundred of these trees, and they all have special names. Passing four, standing in a square called the Sentinels, we saw others called New York, Philadelphia, Boston, Chicago, and there are also very many named after celebrated men. Then our stage coach drove through one living tree called Wawona, 28 feet in diameter. The tree does not appear to have suffered any injury from this large archway having been cut through it.

On reaching Latrop, we re-ascended our Pullman car on the railway, which was afterwards switched on a side line at Berenda station, where we slept; and in the early morning were on our way to Sacramento.

This town lies in a very fertile part of California, and is surrounded by fruit orchards and vineyards. We soon commenced to leave this beautiful valley and ascend the snow clad range of the Sierras Nevadas, passing under large wooden snow sheds, built to protect the line from being blocked by snow. One of these sheds must have been over 20 miles in length; and we could only perceive, through small crevices here and there, some of the glories of the grand mountains we were passing. We spent one whole night and one day on board the train, travelling through the inhospitable state of Nevada, with nothing but prairie land covered with brush to be observed. This large state has only 40,000 inhabitants. Rounding the north end of the Great Salt lake, whose waters are so full of brine that one cannot sink in them, we arrived at five o'clock in the evening at Ogden, 800 miles from San Francisco, where we changed cars for Salt Lake City, the home of the Mormons, which was reached about eight o'clock. Going to the Knutsford hotel, we, as well as the other passengers were curtly informed that it was too late to obtain anything to eat whatever; so we sallied forth, and found a second rate restaurant. I simply mention this as an example of how American independence chooses to assert itself, even at the risk of offending customers.

The next morning, May 26th, we visited Brigham Young's interesting grave; the man who was the introducer of polygamy to the Mormon sect, under the designation of "spiritual wives." The local guide book blazes forth as follows, with regard to this grave :—"thousands visit in appreciative mood this sacred locality, where all that was mortal of the great leader, who has been likened unto Moses, waits the trump of resurrection."

The tomb is a plain white slab of marble, surrounded by an iron palisading, standing in a small cemetery planted with turf. Close to it stands the celebrated bee-hive house, surmounted by a representation of a bee-hive, one of the residences of President Brigham Young and his extensive family, and near it is the celebrated tabernacle, capable of holding 10,000 people. The exterior is exceedingly ugly, and the interior quite plain, free from ornamentation of any kind. At the western end stood a fine carved-wood organ, the largest in America, and in front of this were ranged 250 seats for the choir, and four rows of chairs for the members of the assembly, for whose comfort separate cuspidals were also provided. The building has most remarkable acoustic properties; a pin dropped on to the floor at one end we could hear plainly at the other.

Situated in the same enclosure, and surrounded by a high stone wall, is the temple, lately completed, which has been in course of erection during the last forty years.

Architecturally it has no merit whatever, as it presents the appearance of a large building, made of white granite, suitable for offices; it has three rows of windows on each side, and three towers adorn each end of the roof, one of them being a representation of a Mormon angel in gold, 13 feet high. The building, however, stands out prominently above the city, and is a characteristic landmark.

Among the thirteen articles of faith of this community, as handed down by the founder, number ten is of special interest, viz.:—

"We believe in the literal gathering of Israel, and in the restoration of the ten tribes. That Zion will be built upon this continent. That Christ will reign personally upon this earth, and that the earth will be renewed, and receive its paradisaic glory."

Leaving the sacred precincts of the abode of Mormons, considerably edified, we strolled down one of the broad, handsome streets of the city, and stopped at the theatre, also erected by Brigham Young. Here we discovered that a reception was being held, with gratuitous admission, by the friends and supporters of the Keely Institute. This beneficent institution has for its object the reclamation of confirmed drunkards and those addicted to the tobacco (I presume, both chewing and smoking) and opium habits.

Upon the stage several gentlemen, as well as a little fair haired girl, were sitting in arm chairs, and they were surrounded by wooden easels, holding photographs of celebrities, or special heroes, connected with the undertaking.

There was also a little black poodle dog, which acted as messenger, bringing in occasional notes or telegraphic messages. After a short explanatory address by the chairman, a hidden band struck up,—"Yankee Doodle," "Down upon the Swanee River," and other harmonious national melodies, after which, several "graduates" were requested to come forward and relate their experiences of their several cures, accompanying their painful recitals by copious libations of iced water.

Loud cries were then made for a third individual, whose name I have unfortunately mislaid, who rose and eloquently and graphically described his past ruined home life for forty years, and then the change that had already taken place during the fortnight that he had been under the cure; the happy, smiling faces of his wife and children, and his own altered feelings and habits.

The cure consists of the injection of bromide of gold into the arm, and the institute has homes in most of the large cities of America.

The Great Salt Lake is situated eighteen miles from the city, and is ninety miles long, the waters being as has already been stated, so full of concentrated brine, that it is impossible to drown in them; and bathing is therefore much in vogue at a spot called Garfield beach. The city itself is surrounded by spurs of the Wasutch range of mountains, and is commanded by a fort called Fort George. It is laid out at right angles, and presents the usual dreadful sameness and newness common to all American cities.

Salt Lake City stands at the very threshold of the Rocky mountains, which we now proceeded to cross by the Rio Grande railway, *en route* to the city of Denver. This line is called the "scenic of the world," and the broad gauge track runs through romantic gorges, mountains, and canons, past rushing rivers and upland valleys, surrounded by bare, precipitous mountain peaks. Travelling eastward, one first enters the stupendous canon of the grand river, and the train winds upward through the narrow gorge with its vertical crags of castellated appearance towering on all sides.

We then entered a canon, called King Solomon's temple, and slowly ascended to an altitude of 10,000 feet. Passing Leadville, an important silver mining centre, and Glenwood springs, famous for its hot mineral baths, we shortly afterwards arrived at the Royal gorge, the grandest canon of the Rockies, down which the train rushed.

This pass is so narrow that the railway

track is hewn out of solid rock, by the side of the foaming river. The steep cliffs frowned down upon us, and almost hid the light of day from our view. The American railway guide books are very strong with their description of this really beautiful pass, and I give an extract here :—

"No words can enable the imagination to realize the stupendous and gloomy grandeur of the scene. It is as if the Almighty in his wrath had riven the mountain asunder to make a sepulchre for the sun. And the ancient sun as the centuries roll away into the ocean of time comes, every day a little while, and shines into the great abyss, calmly and pensively, like a passing martyr smiling into his own grave." "The spectacle is a majestic lamentation, and moves the heart to silence and to pity, like a queen's tears."

After this poetic and puffing effusion, the guide books proceed to business by recording the interesting fact that four trans-continental trains pass through this canon every day in the year.

As we passed through Eagle river canon we noticed, 2000 feet above us, a silver mining town perched right up on the cliffs, down which little tramways, with buckets, convey the ore to the trains.

The most beautiful mountain is that of the "Holy Cross," so called because under its summit the snow lies in two deep crevasses exactly in the form of a cross, which can be seen for many miles :—

> "The Holy Cross of Christian faith, above the royal velvet
>> In beauty shines; an emblem wraith high on the beetling helmet!
>> Its white arms, stretching through the sheen of silvery mist, are gleaming—
>> A talisman, the world to screen; Hope's symbol in its seeming!
>> A wonder grand, a joy serene, upon the ages beaming." VISCHER.

In a few hours after leaving the gorge, we arrived at the new bright city of Denver, passing Pueblo en route (once belonging to Mexico).

Denver is situated 4,000 feet above the sea, not far from the foot-hills of the Rockies, whose snow-clad, cloud-kissed mountains seemed quite close, although 30 miles away.

This city is only thirty years of age, and already presents the appearance of a great, prosperous, capital city. Its sudden rise and advancement is due, principally, to its being the centre of the great mining industries of Colorado. It has 160,000 inhabitants, and is built upon a fertile plain, with the summit of Pike's peak a few miles away.

It possesses a splendid opera house, modern theatres, and fire-proof hotels, one of which, known as the "Brown Palace Hotel," is a marvel. It is built entirely of stone and iron, the interior entrance hall being in the form of an octagon, the walls of which are ornamented with mica and onyx. There are four elevators, one of which is used exclusively for the large dining hall, which is situated on the eighth floor, and commands a bird's-eye view of the city, and of the mountains for 300 miles. This building cost 1,000,000 dollars and was built by Mr. Brown on the land on which he settled thirty years previously. In this hotel are all the ultra-modern surprises that the American delights in. The bed in one's bedroom shuts up into a chest of drawers. Each room has separate lavatory and bath room while electric discs placed against the wall give any ordinary requirements usually demanded by visitors, and by moving a pointer the demand is supplied from a central office. Our stay in this city was very pleasant as we were fortunate enough in having introductions to some American gentlemen who specially introduced us to others, the usual formula of introduction being very novel. " Mr. Smith I want you to shake hands with Mr. P—— Mr. Smith said he was proud to shake hands with Mr. P——." If we had stayed much longer we should soon have shaken hands with all the population of Denver, so we thought discretion the better part of valour, and departed by the night Pullman car vestibuled train for the city of Chicago. Journeying on board a train across the continent of America is very similar to ocean travelling. One's fellow passengers are very friendly. Each train has a corridor running through its entire length. There are dining cars, smoking rooms, lavatories, and a great deal of card playing is indulged in by those who like to play, and the time passes very speedily. Each sleeping

Pullman has accommodation for twenty people and the difficulty of travelling is made as luxurious as possible.

May 31*st.*—After two nights we arrived in the City of the West, and drove to the Auditorium Hotel.

The Auditorium is one of America's greatest show buildings, and is proudly called by them the Colosseum of the New World. It is a stately pile, built of massive stone like a Florentine palace, and it comprises a huge hotel, a large theatre, and sets of shops and offices. The dining room is on the eighth floor, and has a view of Michigan avenue and the blue waters of Lake Michigan. The traffic in and out of the central hall resembles that of a railway station. Chicago boasts of possessing the highest inhabited buildings in the world, which are called sky scrapers. The most noticeable of these is the Masonic temple, twenty stories in height, with sixteen elevators, etc. Round the city there are continuous boulevards and parks. Lincoln park has a bronze statue of Abraham Lincoln, and an equestrian one of President Grant. Jackson park is of course covered with the colossal buildings of the World's Fair and here we soon found ourselves. This park is eight miles from the city, and one is conveyed there, either by the elevated railroad, cable or electric cars, by the special service of express trams, laid down along the shores of the lake, or by excursion steamers; so there need be no difficulty of locomotion for the visitors swarming into the city from all parts of the world.

"Chicagoans" have named the Exposition, the "White City," as the beautiful palaces are all of pure classical architecture, of the Italian Renaissance style, in white, and are surrounded by lagoons, canals and lakes with wooded islands, which are reached by rustic bridges. Under the bridges, and over the lakes, dash small electric launches, which are largely used for conveyance about the grounds; as are also gondolas rowed by real Venetian gondoliers. Approaching by steamer on lake Michigan, the White City has an enchanting appearance; and one might easily imagine the mammoth building to have been raised by the waving of a magician's wand, rather than by the work of human creatures. In front of the Golden Dome of the Administration Building is a beautiful lake, at the far end of which the gilded statue of Liberty rises out of the water. On the left and right sides stand the palaces of the Liberal Arts and Agriculture, the latter a dome with large groups of statuary, emblematic of rural life. A glorious fountain, surmounted by a model of a Spanish galleon with rowers, and surrounded by lesser studies of mythological character, pours its waters into the lake. Close by are the palaces devoted to machinery, electricity and mining; while beyond, is that assigned to transportation, with a golden gáteway, upon which are suitable words by Bacon and Macaulay.

Going northward along the margin of the lake are Japanese temples upon the long wooded islands. We pass the Music palace, and the Horticultural and Women's buildings. Away across the lake rises the picturesque Fisheries palace, the State of Illinois building, and representative buildings of Norway, Brazil, India, etc. Behind these, on the shores of Lake Michigan, are characteristic French and German buildings, while close to the pier is an unprententious model of an Elizabethan house, used by the committee of the English section. The States all have handsome representative buildings fitted up as clubhouses, with ornamental furniture and carpets, and each one possesses telegraphic and postal offices. These houses are used as resting places by the visitors from the respective states, who invariably sign their names in leviathan visitors' books. Each one of these buildings is an exhibition in itself; the one representative of New York being a replica of the Capitol at Washington; and the California building a model of the ancient Spanish Mission buildings. This latter is filled with a magnificent selection of the wonderful natural products of fruits, etc., from this prolific state. Virginia has erected an exact model of George Washington's house, with interesting relics of the hero.

The Art Palace is a glorious building, with miles of canvasses, representative of the best modern work of the world There is a fine loan collection from the United States, including gems of Greuze, Corot, Millet, Gerome, Alma Tadema, Rosa Bonheur, Constable, etc. The Germans have sent a colossal canvas from the Berlin gallery, the subject of which is typical of the Fatherland, viz.; "Apotheosis of William I." This depicts the Emperor crowned with laurel leaves, and standing on a triumphal car, re-entering Berlin after the war, and followed by his son Frederick; with Bismarck, Moltke, and the general staff. Another is an original picture of the Berlin Congress, and there is a large one of the present Emperor on horse-back. There are many gems in the English section; Leighton's "Garden of the Hesperides," E. Butler's "Roll Call," Millais' "Bubbles." There are three "Alma Tademas," while Lord Brassey sends a Sussex picture, by Vicat Cole.

June 1st to 5th.—The French have a large exhibit of their highly imaginative, and realistic genre, as well as nude studies.

The whole exhibition is surrounded by an elevated intermural electric railway, with open cars; which are lighted by electricity at night. Perhaps the most novel part of the show, for the Americans, is centred in the portion of the Park the called Midway Plaisance. The Midway is a broad boulevard, connecting Jackson and Washington Parks, and this has been turned into a plaisance; hence the title. In this enclosure are all the private exhibits, as well as various villages filled with inhabitants of different parts of the world. There is the ubiquitous street of Cairo, with its lemon sellers, dromedaries and asses; and an Egyptian theatre with its dances, etc., as well as a model of the Temple of Luxor, containing the mummies of the

Pharaohs, and tombs with inscriptions of the early date of 3,000 or 4,000 years before Christ. Near this is a Tunisian bazaar and theatre, and the beating of the tom toms made us enter. We were very edified to find a young fakir dancing himself into a fit, until his eyes rolled wildly, and then devouring a piece of live coal and swallowing glass ware. When he feasted on a live scorpion our enjoyment increased, and went beyond bounds when he allowed a long green adder to fasten itself round his nose, in which position he carried it about the stage. Dancing yet a little more wildly, in order to screw himself up to the requisite courage, he produced a red hot poker, and after lighting a paper with it, he proceeded to beat it with his hands, and then placed his feet on it. As he survived this operation we were not surprised when he produced a sword and threw himself upon its point. Leaving this clever performance, we paid a visit to old Vienna, which was represented by a grouping of old buildings of the Graben, a celebrated market place in that city. Here an Austrian brass band discoursed sweet music, while appreciative Germans sat around and quaffed the local "lager" beer, and one might easily have imagined oneself transported to a typical beer garden. Close by was a Chinese theatre and joss house. Further along a Lapland village, with Laplanders, reindeer, etc.; and a Dahomey village with a tribe of fifty Dahomeyans, who were good enongh to array themselves in grassy costumes to allay the prejudices of their American audience, as they went through the extraordinary evolutions of their war-dance. The Hawaiian Republic exhibited a panorama of the fearful volcano of Kilauea. There were also panoramas of the Paris Exhibition, of the Alps, and of St. Peter's at Rome, in addition to Turkish, Persian, Moorish and Saracenic buildings, all with native bazaars and theatres for the exhibition of their distinctive dances. Then the Germans had erected a real village and old German castle with a moat. Here we dined, and listened to the loud strain of a German brass band, sent by the Fatherland. As there are over 350,000 Germans living in Chicago, the Teutonic element is largely represented at the exhibition, and, indeed the German exhibits are very extensive in all departments. The Irish also had a model of an old castle, with a well, and the blarney stone. Opposite this, the stalwart forms of two bagpipers, discoursing sweet music, called our attention, not to a Scotch exhibit but to the world's congress of beauty. Entering the abode where beauty dwelt, we found the representatives of the divinity ranged on elevated platforms right round a room, and guarded from too close an inspection by an iron rail. Here reposed a Chinese lady, and also Welsh, Scotch, Alsatian, Swiss, Norwegian, Russian, Japanese and German girls. At the extreme end, reclined on a gorgeous couch, Fatima, with a far-away dreamy air, was surrounded by other Turkish maidens, all in languorous attitudes, some of them not disdaining to puff the dainty cigarette. Addressing Fatima, to my surprise I found she was equally conversant with French, German and English languages, and hailed from Vienna. Another lady was attired in a "Worth" gown, and came from Edinburgh. Two Mexican young ladies were attired in decolleté gowns; one was very thin and the other very stout. The latter was reading Lorna Doone, and told me that "she had heard a lot of marquises, dukes and earls were coming to the show; she had not seen them yet, but hoped she would." A young girl attired in a pale green Grecian dress, with a silver band, was very sulky; and with reason, for she was expected to show the loose flowing draperies of her costume by continually promenading; and just as she, perhaps, had reached an interesting part of her novel, she would be requested by an American lady to "stand up, please." This classical young lady did not hail from the Hellenic peninsula, but was a home bred "Chicagoan." The Chinese lady was always peacefully slumbering, and the Japanese one, writing. The Russian young lady spoke German fluently, but said she was from Poland; while the Alsatian came from the Bernese Oberland.

I came away rather mixed up with the cosmopolitan nature of the young ladies exhibited. Opposite to this was Hagenbeck's arena of trained wild animals. Here a wonderful performance takes place daily. The arena is a large cage, in which Mr. Hagenbeck introduces at once, lions, tigers, bears, panthers, lynx, wild boar and boar-hounds, a happy family of wild beasts. After putting them through most extraordinary tricks; one of which consisted of harnessing two Bengal tigers to a Roman chariot, leading a lion attired in a crown and a long ermine robe, behind which were two boars, as pages, and which went round the ring,—the whole of the animals were ranged as a living staircase. One lion also was put through an equestrian performance on the bare back of a horse, jumping through hoops, etc.

A few general facts with regard to the Exposition may not be uninteresting:—

Jackson Park is situated on the shores of Lake Michigan, and embraces 533 acres, while the Midway Plaisance has 80. The structures erected upon these parks, cover twice the area of those of the Paris Exhibition of 1889, and alone they have cost more than fifty per cent. of the total cost of the Paris fair. Five million dollars have been spent in the laying out of the grounds, and the total cost of the Exposition to its close is estimated at 22,000,000 dollars. Seventeen thousand horse-power for electric lighting is provided. This is three times the electric lighting power in use for Chicago, and ten times that provided for the Paris exhibition. The material used in the construction of the buildings is called "staff," together with iron, wood and glass.

Thirty thousand tons of staff were consumed. This was invented in France in 1876, and was first used in the Paris Exhibition of 1878. It is composed chiefly of powdered gypsum, the other constituents being alumina, glycerine and dextrina. These are mixed with water without heat, and cast in moulds in any desired shape, and then allowed to harden. Staff is impervious to water, and is a permanent building material, although it cost is one-tenth that of granite. The cost of the great buildings was eight million dollars.

Landscape gardening cost 323,500 dollars; viaducts and bridges 125,000; grading and filling up, 450,000; piers 70,000; waterway improvements, 225,000; railways, 500,000; steam plant, 800,000; electric lighting, 1,500,000; statutary 1,000,000; vases, lamps, etc. 50,000; lake front adornment, 200,000; sewerage and water supply, 600,000; and sundries, 1,000,000 dollars.

FACTS ABOUT CHICAGO.

Chicago has over one million inhabitants. There are 317 churches, and 150,000 volumes in the public library. Its parks cover 197,461 acres, and its entire area is over 181 square miles. Finest city in the United States, from an architectural stand point.

June 5th, 1893.—Everybody has heard something of the machine, in one end of which live pigs are placed, while sausages come out at the other. This, of course, is a slight exaggeration; but nevertheless, the conversion of hogs into sausages is one of the sights of Chicago; and so we went in due course to the stockyards of Messrs. Armour & Co., where no fewer than 1,750,000 hogs were killed in 1892, as well as

850,000 head of cattle and 600,000 sheep. We were first shown into a large storehouse, where the unfortunate live hogs were hanging in rows, suspended by one hind leg on an inclined plane, and as they moved along in rotation they were promptly "struck" by a blood be-spattered butcher standing underneath. They were then passed on, and dropped into a large trough full of scalding hot water, in which they rolled over and over, until caught up in a machine which literally skinned them. Their heads were then cut off by a dexterous hand. They were then cut up and passed on to the cooling and curing rooms. Each operation was pointed out, until we arrived at the rooms where sausages were being turned out. Here indeed was sausage, miles of sausage, every variety of sausage. Frankfort sausage, Bologna, Wiener Wurst, liver sausage, and blood sausage. Everything was clean and sweet, but the squealing of the pigs still in my memory dwells!

The cattle are killed by being hammered on the head by a man.

June 7th.—We proceeded by rail, along the shores of Lakes Michigan and Erie, to Buffalo, in fifteen hours. Here we changed cars and arrived at Niagara in an hour. As the finest views of the waterfall are on the Canadian side, we crossed the suspension bridge thrown across the gorge about 200 feet above the water, and passed into Canada, where we put up at the Clifton House. The noise of the falling mass of waters could be heard from a great distance, and from our window the American fall could plainly be seen. The more important is called the Horse Shoe. Clouds of white mist rise from the deep abyss at the bottom and effectually hide the tumult of seething waters from sight. One can only hear a dull roaring sound like a far away battle. The whole effect of this terrific volume of down-pouring waters is truly awe-inspiring, and difficult to describe. A small steamer called the "Maid of the Mist" approaches as near as possible until driven back by the velocity of the current, while the sight-seer on board, enveloped in thick waterproof clothing, is almost blinded by the showers of falling spray.

Along the American bank a town has been built and a large paper mill rears itself in all its ugliness along the bank; but on the Canadian side, a beautiful park, called "The Queen Victoria," has been tastefully laid out. At the top of the cliff an electric car service has lately been established, and these cars run for a distance of three miles from the falls (and past the foaming rapids where Captain Webb lost his life,) to the whirlpool, giving one a superb view of the romantic gorge.

Above the falls there is a drop from the waters of Lake Erie of fifty feet, forming a cataract, resembling a terrace of surf, preparatory to the final plunge. Beautiful peeps of these falling waters can be obtained from the islands called the Three Sisters, connected by wooden bridges on the American side, and the Dufferin islands on the Canadian.

June 9th.—Leaving the falls by train, we arrived in half an hour at Niagara by the lake, where we stepped on board the steamer " Chicory," and passing between the two forts of Niagara and Massagawa we were soon crossing a portion of the Lake Ontario, and arrived in a couple of hours at the city of Toronto.

After a drive through the broad and evenly built streets, and having admired the blossoming chestnut trees which grew in profusion; we paid a visit to the English cathedral of St. James, and then departed by steamer, "Passport" for the Thousand islands, and rapids of the river St. Lawrence, and for Montreal. On the morning of the 10th, we entered the river and were soon gliding in and out of the islands, some of which are simply small rocks, with a few trees upon them, and others beautifully wooded, and with sloping green banks. On many of them large hotels have been built, and the whole neighbourhood, because of its romantic picturesqueness and excellent fishing, is becoming much visited and increasingly popular with holiday-seeking Americans. The navigation of the stream is very difficult because of its swift current and the rapids, which the steamers now descend.

The first of these are the Long Sault rapids. The vessel plunged down them as if she was settling into the water, while the current tore along at the rate of twenty miles an hour.

Looking backward, it appeared as if we had slipped over a solid bed of submerged rocks. After passing through one or two minor rapids, not so exciting, the river broadened to a fine lake, at the end of which we sailed under a large railway bridge of the Canadian Pacific Railway, and the city of Montreal came into view. Just before reaching it, however, the Lachine rapids, which are the most exciting of the trip, have to be shot. Here the water rose and fell like ocean billows, and as the big steamer raced down the slope, with here and there an occasional bit of brown rock projecting out of the waters, the foam dashed over us as if we were sailing in the teeth of a gale. We were past the danger in three minutes.

The city of Montreal is quite French in character, and two-thirds of the inhabitants are French Canadians. Just behind the city rises a wooded hill called Mount Royal, from which the city derives its name. The Roman Catholic clergy have many churches in the city; the most interesting being a large replica of St. Peter at Rome, and a copy of Notre Dame in Paris. There are also large numbers of modern churches, belonging to Presbyterians, Methodists, etc., as well as a handsome cathedral of the Anglican church. The older quarters of the city are all named after French saints, and after quarters of Paris; St. Francis, St. Genevieve, St. Antoine, St. Denis, etc. The older houses are also all in French style, with jalousies and gabled windows in the roofs. The language spoken is mostly French, but it is unfortunately spoken with an accent more Breton or Norman in style, and is difficult of comprehension.

A winding carriage road conducts one to the summit of Mount Royal, from which a view of the city immediately beneath, and the far reaching expanse of the waters of the St. Lawrence, is enjoyed.

The voyage to Quebec is usually accomplished during the night, by means of large, palatially fitted steamers; and embarking therefore on board the "Quebec," we were the next morning under the memorable heights of Quebec, scaled so gallantly by Wolff. Quebec is decidedly French. Old fashioned lanes and streets nestle under the fort, which has been named the Gibraltar of America. One might be in sunny France. Old fashioned Roman Catholic churches, nunneries, etc., abound. A curious two-wheeled conveyance, called a calêche, is the usual carriage; and mounting one of these we were driven to the fort, to the monument on the height of Abraham, marking the spot where Wolff fell; and to the Parliament house, adorned with busts of both French and English soldiers and statesmen.

Driving through French Canadian villages, we came to the falls of Montmorency, about ten miles distant. This beautiful cascade falls 250 feet into a basin, surrounded by wooded hills, close to the St. Lawrence river. On the opposite bank stretch the Laurentian hills for many miles, while the picturesque white cottages of the peasants are seen peeping out of the bright green woods, at intervals, along the banks of the stream; and away to the right, on a promontory, we could see the city of Quebec.

Returning to Montreal we paid a flying visit by train to Ottawa, to see the handsome modern Houses of Parliament of the Canadian Government, which are erected on a hill above the city. Handsome oil paintings of the former Viceroys adorned the corridors, while in the library was a large octagonal structure, containing many thousands of both French and English books. Returning to Montreal again we took rail to Plattsburgh, and then proceeded by steamer down Lakes Champlain and George, obtaining distant views of the Adirondack hills—to Saratoga Springs, one of America's gayest watering places. Besides the mineral baths and springs, this Spa, which resembles Wiesbaden, is celebrated for its monster wooden hotels and the salubrity of its air. It is embowered in trees under which hundreds of wooden villas are built, which are frequented by Americans, who are driven away from their cities by the intense heat during the months of July and August. From Saratoga a short railway trip brought us to Albany on the shores of the far-famed Hudson river, called the "American Rhine," (but only by Americans), where the steamer "Albany," conveyed us down stream to New York city. The river is of course much broader than the Rhine, but it lacks the beauty of the romantic ruined castles and villages, added to which its natural charm is utterly destroyed by the hundreds of cheap trippers from New York who overcrowd the boats; the girls chewing and sucking a gum sweetmeat called tutti-frutti, and candies, and the men with their odious expectorating habits.

New York is built, as all the world knows, upon Manhattan Island; and is connected with the mainland by large ferry boats, and with

Brooklyn by the high suspension bridge. Most of the railway termini are in Jersey city. On a small rock at the entrance of the harbour stands the colossal figure of "Liberty," by Bartholdi; given by France to her sister republic. Broadway is the principal street of shops; it is of immense length and has great traffic; but the Fifth Avenue is the most handsome street, and is composed of palatial hotels, clubs, churches and private residences. At its western end commences the fine Central Park of 900 acres, where we heard a selection of classical music on Sunday afternoon, which was listened to by a crowd of fully 10,000 promenaders. A great many of the other broad avenues are ruined by the ugliness of the elevated railroads which are built upon iron columns right down the centres of the streets, while electric cars ply underneath. There is only one thing to be said in favour of these means of transportation, and that is, that it would be impossible for New York to do without them. They are built on the level of the first floor windows, and cause the greatest inconvenience to the inhabitants along the line of route by the smoke of the engines blowing into the windows, and by the noise of the trains passing every two minutes. In some thoroughfares the trains actually run over the pavements. The Roman Catholic cathedral of St. Patrick is a handsome white stone building of Gothic architecture, with two tapering spires 350 feet high, and handsome coloured glass windows. This church, as well as the Anglican one, is on Fifth Avenue. New York possesses many modern theatres, and the greatest novelty of these is that some of them are provided with open air garden roofs, lighted brilliantly by the electric light, where music hall

(352)

variety entertainments are given. Admission to the theatres is inclusive of a pass to the garden, to which one is conveyed by elevators. Iced water and Japanese fans are presented free by the management to the visitors. Upon Madison square stands one building, containing a theatre and an immense amphitheatre, capable of holding 20,000 people.

One of the great Sunday rendezvous of New Yorkers is Coney Island, about an hour's distance by steamboat. On these sands indiscriminate bathing is indulged in, while hundreds of variety-chorus dancing booths, shooting galleries, circular toboggan slides and switchbacks afford amusement. The whole place is a kind of glorified Derby day, with the unpleasant attractions of music hall stages, upon which white girls and niggers were singing and dancing. To have wafted Mr.

Z———, of L———, here for a few hours one Sunday afternoon would have made him cold with fright. Above the booths towered a colossal model of an elephant, two hundred feet high.

The city of Washington was next visited. Washington is the home of the Administrative Governmental Buildings of the United States and of the President. The buildings are entirely of white stone, and are of classical architecture. The Capitol stands on a hill, and is visible all over the city. Its rotunda is very handsome and the interior is embellished with a handsome frieze, underneath which are large paintings of events in American history. The Washington tower is the highest permanent structure in the world, 500 feet high, 40 feet higher than the tower of Cologne Cathedral.

An elevator takes one to a height of 500

feet. The White House is an unpretentious building, with one handsome reception room, in which those persons desirous of paying their respects to President Cleveland are permitted to do so. We were desirous, and had the pleasure of shaking hands. Close to the White House are the Treasury, and the Army and Navy buildings; and in the library of the latter we read the original manuscript copy of the Charter of Independence. Washington's fine broad streets are lined with avenues of trees, and are quiet and provincial in style as compared with the larger and more populous cities of Chicago, New York, or Philadelphia. This latter city has about $1\frac{1}{4}$ millions of inhabitants and stands on the banks of the river Schuylkill, which is frequented by oarsmen, like our own silvery Thames.

Independence Hall is its only historical building, containing the famous Liberty Bill, now removed for exhibition to the World's Fair. You may look in vain for a crooked street in Philadelphia, as the city is laid out exactly in chessboard pattern, and contains handsome sky-scraping buildings, as well as a magnificent pile of buildings known as the City Hall, the tower of which is not yet completed.

Returning to New York we went by the Limited Express, and ran the 235 miles to Boston in four hours. Boston is old fashioned, and actually has the audacious novelty of crooked streets, and old English houses, with bulging bay windows. The streets are thronged, however, with processions of electric cars which run to the suburbs of Cambridge, Chelsea, etc., etc.

Bunkers Hill rises in the centre of the suburb of Charleston, and is commemorated by a stone obelisk. The city hall has a gilded dome from which a splendid view of the city and the harbour is obtained. At Cambridge the Harvard University is to be seen.

July 1st.—Last evening we embarked on board the Cunard Company's new steamship (sister ship to the "Lucania") "Campania" of 12,600 tons, and engines of 30,000 horse power, to make the run home across the "Herring Pond." This ship is the largest ocean-going steamer in the world and possesses two funnels, twenty feet in diameter, the largest ever constructed. There are five decks; and on the main deck the music saloon, the library and smoking room, as well as a great many state rooms, are constructed. The smoking room is of carved oak, and actually possesses a fire-grate, which is lighted during cold winter passages. The ship is 700 feet long, and cost over £600,000.

July 2nd, Sunday.—We have had rather an exciting day. A waterspout, a whale, and four ships were sighted. On board "Commander" Ballington Booth held a Salvationist meeting, and two revivalist lectures were given. Then the captain read the burial service over the body of a passenger, who died suddenly of an apoplectic stroke, and was buried in the ocean.

CONCLUSION.

July 7th.—Our voyage home, like most of the Atlantic crossings, has been an uneventful one.

Running up the Irish Channel in foggy weather we soon reached the broad estuary of the Mersey, and shortly after disembarked from our steamer to the small steam tender which came alongside and conveyed us to one of the landing stages at Liverpool. Passing the night at the Grand Hotel, Liverpool, we proceeded the following morning to London, having accomplished our voyage round the world in just upon seven months.

It is a curious feeling, that of returning home to familiar scenes after a long absence, during which many places have been visited. We had left London amid the bitter cold of December, and returned to find the City in all the blaze of July sunshine. Yet how quickly we seem to slip into the old scenes and surroundings. How difficult it seems even after a few hours to realise that a week ago we were in New York, a month ago at Chicago, and three months ago almost to the day we were just arriving at Yokohama, having visited China, India and other countries.

And now, as we once more mingle with London life, the scenes we have visited seem to vanish from our memories with astonishing rapidity; until we sometimes wonder whether our visit to these wonderful spots is not a dream instead of an actual event of recent occurrence. At such times as these we slip away and look at our diary, and then as we turn its pages again, the beauties of Ceylon—the vegetation of Colombo—the temples of India—the sights of China—the delights of happy Japan—and the wonders of the Yosemite Valley—all seem in imagination once more to pass in welcome procession before us.

APPENDIX.

OF BUDDHA AND BUDDHISM.

THE word Buddha comes from Budh, to know; and the founder of Buddhism was named Gautama, who claimed to be Sarvagnya, omniscient, to know all things; and the religion which he established was a "proud attempt to create a faith without a God, and to conceive a deliverance in which man delivers himself."

Buddha, in Burmese is generally called "Phra," in Chinese "Fo"; but when he lived is very uncertain, as many different dates are given. In Ceylon, he is supposed to have lived 543 years before the Christian Era, and died at the age of 80. He was born in Kapilavastu, a town about 100 miles north of Benares. His father, " Suddhodana," (one possessed of pure rice) was ruler of the Sakya tribe, and his mother, Moya, was childless till her forty-fifth year. At his birth, he took seven steps forward, a lotus springing up at each step, and said, with a loud voice, "I am the most excellent in the world, I am the chief of the world, hereafter there is to me no other birth."

On the fifth day he was called Siddhartha, "he who has accomplished his aim." His mother died within a week, and his sister Mahapajapati, became his foster-mother. In his sixteenth year, he was married to Yasodhara, daughter of the king of Koli. Besides her, he is said to have had 40,000 concubines, and singing women. Till his twenty-ninth year, Siddhartha lived in the full enjoyment of every kind of pleasure, when he altered his life and became an ascetic. For six years he then gave himself to the most severe penances, until he became so weak, that he fell senseless to the ground, and was supposed to be dead. After preaching for forty-five years he was attacked by a severe and painful illness, to which he eventually succumbed.

Throughout his public life, Gautama was in the habit of travelling about most of the fine parts of the year, preaching to the people; but during the rainy months in North India from June to October, he remained in one place, devoting himself more particularly to the instruction of his disciples. Unlike the Brahmins, Gautama admitted into the priesthood persons of all castes. His followers had an easy life, and were treated with respect. In course of time, he gained a large number of adherents, and at one time he was joined by a thousand fire-worshippers, disciples of Kasypa. His last words to his "followers," were :—

"Behold now, brethren, I exhort you saying, decay is inherent in all component things. Work out, with diligence, your own perfection."

Shortly afterwards he passed away, in an unconscious state. A grand funeral pile was prepared by the Mallas of Kusinara, but it would not burn till Moha Kasyapa had come with 500 priests, and worshipped at the feet of Buddha. Then the pile caught fire of itself. When the body was consumed, torrents of water from above, and beneath, extinguished the flames. The bones that remained, were taken, with a grand procession, to the city, where they were afterwards distributed. Buddhism is confined to Eastern Asia, and in no country does it exist alone. Demon worship was the original superstition in Ceylon, and has a far greater hold upon the people than Buddhism. The worship of the Hindoo gods was introduced by the kings. In some of their charms, the Singhalese mix the names of Buddha, Brahma, Vishnu, and demons. In Ceylon, there are two Buddhist sects, the Siamese and Burmese. The latter, introduced about the beginning of the present century, requires priests to cover both shoulders with their robes, and leave the eyebrows unshorn. They claim greater purity than the Siamese sect, condemning the worship of the Hindoo gods.

Gautama rests his claim to be the greatest of beings, mainly in his alleged omniscience. He was supposed to know all things, past, present, and to come. Hence he is called Buddha, the enlightened one; Sarvagnya, the all-wise; and Samma-sam-Buddha, the completely enlightened one. This knowledge, he says, was self-acquired and not derived from any one. In the Mahavagga, he says: "I am the all-knowing—by my own power I possess knowledge. Whom should I call my master? I have no teacher." When he preached his first sermon, it is said that the foundations of 10,000 worlds were shaken, and a brilliant light was presented. In illustration of Buddha's kindness, it is said, that in his various births (550 of them) he sacrificed himself so often to provide food for hungry wild beasts and demons, that he gave more eyes than there are stars in the heavens, more blood than there is water in the four oceans, and more flesh than there is earth in all the continents of the world.

THE DOCTRINES OF BUDDHA.*

1st. The denial of a Creator. Gautama did not expressly say that there is no Creator, but he implied it when he claimed to be the greatest being in the universe,—and he discouraged inquiry, because he wished himself to be regarded as the greatest being,—to be worshipped instead of the great Creator of the universe.

2nd. Denial of an intelligent Governor of the world. Instead of a great Creator governing the world which he has made, Buddhism substitutes Karma. The word Karma comes from Kri, to do, and means "doing or act." It denotes the moral quality of an action, whether good or evil. Human beings partake of their own Karma; Karma

---

* Extracts from a pamphlet issued by a Madras Educational Society and from information given me by a priest.

apportions to beings, prosperity or adversity. Budda teaches that the merit or demerit of actions produces evil or good to men, without the intervention of a judge to decide on that merit or demerit, or of a person to give to the individual either the reward or the punishment.

3rd. No hearer of prayer. Man is his own god. Buddhism proclaims a salvation which each man is to gain for himself, and by himself, in this world during this life, without the least reference to God or to gods, great or small. Buddha himself cannot hear prayer He has entered "Nirvana," and is now existent. There is no help. Every misfortune must be endured. There is no pardon of sin. Punishments of sin are most appalling, but no cry for mercy can be heard.

4th. Man has no soul. Buddha's doctrine is that there is no soul in man which transmigrates, but that the whole of a man ceases at death. Buddhists, in general believe that a man has a body and a soul; that upon the death of the body the soul enters into some other body, and in that new body it is either rewarded or punished for the actions performed by the said soul after a previous birth.

5th. No permanent happiness.

PRECEPTS.

1st. Not to take life.

2nd. Not to steal.

3rd. Not to commit adultery.

4th. Not to tell lies.

5th. Not to drink intoxicating liquors.

Three other commands are sometimes taken.

6th. Not to eat after noon.

7th. Not to attend dancing, stage plays, etc.

8th. Not to use perfumes.

Priests are bound to use two more.

9th. Not to use high beds or couches.

10th. Not to receive gold or silver.

THE THREEFOLD REFUGE.

There are three refuges in the Buddhist religion, called—the threefold refuge, viz :—

1st. Buddha has a refuge. Buddha claims to be a refuge on account of his supposed wisdom and greatness, and that is one reason why his supposed relics are worshipped. At Kandy is a golden shrine at which the people do reverence before his left canine tooth; which is supposed to have sustained wonderful trials. When thrown into a burning furnace, it appeared on the surface of a lotus. An attempt was made to crush it on an anvil, but it remained embedded in the iron, resisting all the means employed to take it out, until Subadda, a Buddhist, got it removed. These stories are devoid of truth:—

Let the relic now be tested on an anvil.

Pilgrimages are made to the top of Adam's Peak, where there is supposed to be a footprint of Buddha; but there is only a little hollow in the rock, and the likeness to the foot is made with chunam or lime; and is a gross deception.

Images of Buddha have honor paid to them. His height was eighteen cubits; but how could a man eighteen cubits high have a wife less than four? How could he have entered ordinary dwellings? In Japan one image represents him as thirty-two cubits high.

2nd. The doctrines as a refuge (as described on page 364).

3rd. The priesthood as a refuge.

The spread of Buddhism is largely owing to the priesthood. The Brahmins confined the office to their own caste, but Gautama freely admitted all. Priests were required to submit to certain rules, but they had not to toil for their living. Buddha claimed for the priests the honor due to himself;—once a year the King of Siam makes formal obeisance to the priesthood. A priest in Ceylon was asked,

"Do you worship the gods?" "No" said he, "the gods worship me." To show the greatness of Buddha, and thus of themselves, the priests who wrote the sacred books attributed the most astonishing miracles to him. Gifts to the priesthoods were said to confer great merit upon the donor. All these were encouragements to enter the priesthood, and motives to spread the religion.

www.ingramcontent.com/pod-product-compliance
Lightning Source LLC
Chambersburg PA
CBHW030345230426
43664CB00007BB/540